The married homosexual man

To Peter, who thought I should have been gardening instead.

The married homosexual man

A psychological study

Michael W. Ross

Routledge & Kegan Paul
London, Boston, Melbourne and Henley

First published in 1983
by Routledge & Kegan Paul plc
39 Store Street, London WC1E 7DD,
9 Park Street, Boston, Mass. 02108, USA,
296 Beaconsfield Parade, Middle Park,
Melbourne, 3206, Australia, and
Broadway House, Newtown Road,
Henley-on-Thames, Oxon RG9 1EN
Printed in Great Britain by
TJ Press Ltd, Padstow, Cornwall

Library of Congress Cataloging in Publication Data

Ross, Michael W., 1952-

The married homosexual man.
Bibliography: p.
Includes index.
1. Homosexuals, Male. 2. Married people.
3. Husbands.
HQ76.R65   1983   306.7'662   83-8666

ISBN 0-7100-9532-5

'he asked to interview me, for The Book, but I told him my affairs with the angels are too precious to reduce them to lines on a graph!'

John Rechy, *City of Night*

Contents

Contents

Foreword

In 1978, the National Gay Task Force compiled a variety of scientific data and, extrapolating from it, 'guestimated' that one in every five American families has a homosexual member. The figure is surprisingly large and raises an obvious question: Why, if homosexuality is so common, has it been so invisible? Ross's unique research details one possible answer — the homosexual family member is often the one least suspected, the husband.

Unique research like this requires unique methodology, and the legacy of homosexual research exemplifies many creative approaches. Bell, Weinberg and Hammersmith (*Sexual Preference*), Harry and Devall (*The Social Organization of Gay Males*), and Weinberg and Williams (*Male Homosexuals*) employ survey research and hypothesis testing methods. Wold (*The Lesbian Community*), Harris (*The Dilly Boys*) and Humphreys (*Tearoom Trade*) use anthropological and ethnographic techniques. The Adairs (*Word is Out*) show the value of face-to-face interviews. Psychoanalytic methods are employed by Stoller (*Sex and Gender*). Spada (*The Spada Report*) and Jay and Young (*The Gay Report*) use anonymous questionnaires. Russo (*The Celluloid Closet*) and White (*States of Desire*) use movie data and travel diaries respectively. Autobiographical approaches are favoured by Boyd (*Take Off the Masks*) and Isherwood (*Christopher and his Kind*). Boswell (*Christianity, Social Tolerance and Homosexuality*) and Katz (*Gay American History*) employ historical data.

Ross, however, employs the unusual combination of

ix

anonymous questionnaires, hypotheses testing, and psychiatric interviews with respondents in three countries. In doing so, he brings together information that contributes to establishing the psychology of sex behaviour on a theoretically and methodologically sound basis. His innovative approach also has the advantage of providing both quantitative and qualitative data. Quantitative data have the benefit of being reasonably straightforward and, in this relatively unexplored field of gay husbands, they provide a broad overview of some of the fundamental issues: What distinquishes gays who marry from those who do not? Are gay-straight marriages stable or divorce-prone? What differentiates those who stay married from those who do not? Qualitative data, on the other hand, tell what if *feels* like to be a gay husband. This material is contained especially in the chapters on implications for therapy where examples and applications of the findings address the pain of gay married men. The confluence of the two data sets provides a more complete understanding of gay husbands than either data set could by itself.

On such a passionately sensitive topic as gay married men, Ross's study demonstrates the scientific virtue of quiet concern for the truth, the facts of the matter. He reports the findings in a clear, direct, low-key manner. Ross wisely indicates the techniques needing refinements and the cautions essential in interpreting the data. He shows the reader exactly the process of his thinking so that we can also evaluate the results. And he marks the paths yet to be travelled, the questions remaining. For example, the perspectives of the men's wives, children and gay lovers are fascinating areas that remain unexplored.

In spite of its dedication to the scientific method, the book is not without its politics. Simply by documenting the lives of gay husbands, the data question assumptions that gay males are out to destroy marriage and family life, that they necessarily hate women and shun them. The data also show the extent to which some homosexuals have internalised anti-gay prejudice and, in attempting to flee this hostility, have been duped into self-hatred and stifling themselves in nuptial closets. This study, moreover, exposes the ideology of moral entrepreneurs and other agents of social conformity. Such people prescribe that homosexuals get married, settle down family style, fit in, and that they will be cured. Ross's respondents report to the contrary — during marriage their gay feelings did not diminish but intensified.

In the latter part of the book, Ross takes the knowledge gained from his survey and shows how it can help individuals live happier lives. In doing so, he joins a tradition that emphasises the contributions of the scientist to policy and professional practice. This tradition is not based on contrived research or simplistic popularisation. Reasoned and responsible scholarship leads to empirical findings and to the formulation of delimited generalisations. It is hoped that such results are relevant for all interested in counselling and policy issues. This book is no plea for utopia based on research to be completed in the distant future, but rather a contribution to immediate understanding.

Brian Miller
Claremont Graduate School,
Claremont, California.

Preface

The idea for a study of homosexual men who marry was born in a discussion with Stewart Ransom of Massey University and Rev. Dr Felix Donnelly of the University of Auckland when, as a 23-year-old postgraduate student, I was looking for a thesis topic in the area of homosexuality which did not deal with etiology, would provide information which could be of some practical use, and was in an area not previously heavily researched. After discarding the idea of looking at older homosexuals and their adjustment, I raised the issue of the married homosexual, which we all felt was worth looking at.

The result was the production of a thesis which is embodied, hopefully, in a less technical and turgid form, in the first study reported in this book, and which also lead to the production of several brief scientific papers reporting aspects of the results. However, the lack of any subsequent scientific research on the question of why homosexual men marry and what happens to them and their marriages provided a stimulus to write the whole study up as a monograph in order to relate the factors involved in the marriage of homosexual men to one another without the constraints imposed by the form of scientific papers.

After completing this work and going on to a doctorate, I maintained a residual interest in the issue of married homosexual men, and in the course of further field work at the Universities of Melbourne and Stockholm where I completed my doctorate, and at the University of Helsinki where I did some post-doctoral research I continued to investigate it.

While this investigation was at a relatively cursory level, it did provide an opportunity to confirm some of the hypotheses raised in the earlier study, and in particular the effects of societal and social environment on the phenomenon. In the years intervening since the completion of my doctoral work in 1978 I had constantly been expecting a major study on married homosexuals to appear, although in fact the number of papers appearing on married homosexual men in that period could almost be counted on the fingers of one hand. As a result, I came to the conclusion, over a period of several months, that in the absence of much additional work on the area, my responsibility as a scientist was to offer my data for publication. In this regard, the encouragement of Dr Lesley Rogers and Helen McCulloch was an additional stimulus. My conclusion was also based on other criteria. I had constantly been surprised at the number of married homosexuals who I had seen in my outpatient clinic, and discussions with colleagues as far afield as Britain, the United States, Finland and Czechoslovakia confirmed this. Not only did the married homosexual men feel that they were the only person in the community with this problem (much as homosexuals felt over ten years ago), but there was also very little guidance for the professional.

As a consequence, I have tried to serve two masters in writing this book: the scientific community in providing my data and analyses, and the helping professions in providing some information and conclusions which may assist them. Hopefully, the scope will stretch beyond even these two broad groups, as this is also intended as a book for the educated lay person. Whether it has succeeded in satisfying such a plethora of aims remains to be seen. However, if it has managed to provide a perspective on the married homosexual man and in particular a contribution to the study of human sexuality, it will have more than served its purpose.

Mike Ross,
Adelaide, South Australia

Acknowledgments

My greatest debt is to all those who are the source of the information contained within this book, but who must remain nameless. A debt of almost the same magnitude is due to those organisations which gave me access to their members through their mailing lists or newsletters, including the New Zealand Homosexual Law Reform Society and Society Five in Melbourne for the first study, and for the second study, Society Five and the Metropolitan Community Church in Melbourne, Camp Inc. and the Metropolitan Community Church in Brisbane, RFSL in Stockholm, and SETA in Helsinki. The second study was itself part of a larger study which was only made possible by two generous travel grants from the Faculty of Arts of the University of Melbourne. The bulk of the information contained in this book is based on a master's thesis in psychology from the Victoria University of Wellington, New Zealand. I am indebted to my supervisors, Professor Tony Taylor, Dr Ngaire Adcock, and Professor C. J. Adcock, for their support of what must have, in 1975, seemed a rather unusual piece of research. The importance of a stimulating and research-oriented environment was no less critical in writing this book in 1982, for which Professor Ross Kalucy and my colleagues in the Department of Psychiatry at the Flinders University Medical School have my gratitude. Similarly, the contribution of Janine Judd, Jane Orange, Jane Tamkin and Sally Munchenberg in typing the manuscript was considerable, for which they have my thanks. Permission to reproduce material was kindly granted by the following publishers: Oxford University Press for permission to reproduce the questionnaire from *Male Homosexuals: Their Problems and Adaptation* by M. S. Weinberg and C. J. Williams; Medical News Tribune for permission to reproduce in part 'Bisexuality: fact or fallacy' by M. W. Ross from the *British Journal of Sexual Medicine*, 1979, 6(45), pp. 49-50; Family Life Movement of Australia for permission to reproduce in part 'Some effects of heterosexual marriage on homosexual desire', by M. W. Ross from the *Australian Journal of Sex, Marriage and Family*, 1982 3(1), pp. 25-30; Human Sciences Press for permission to reproduce 'Heterosexual marriage of homosexual males: some associated factors', by M. W. Ross from the *Journal of Sex and Marital Therapy*, 1979, 5(2), pp. 142-51.

1 Introduction

'All that is left is to pretend. But to pretend to the end of one's life is the highest torment.' So wrote the composer Peter Tchaikovsky following his marriage to his student, Antonina Milyukov, in 1877. How common is such a conclusion amongst males with homosexual tendencies who have married in the century since Tchaikovsky wrote? [Some homosexuals marry. Why they do it, and the consequences of such an act, are still open questions.] Recently some professional counsellors of those male homosexuals with adaptation or adjustment problems have expressed concern at the proportion of heterosexually married homosexuals who seek help. McNeill (1977), for example, reports that one priest who serves as a canon lawyer in a Catholic marriage tribunal contends that in over a third of the divorces with which he has dealt, one of the partners was homosexually inclined, a fact of major disruption for the marriage. While estimates of the proportion of these married homosexual men seeking help range from 10 to 20 per cent of homosexuals, there is agreement that, from the purely professional point of view, the information needed to deal with such clients with any degree of insight is lacking.

To date, it has been widely assumed that homosexual men marry in response to some form of 'social pressure' (that is, the individually perceived strength of a pattern of social stimuli acting upon a person, emphasising conformity to a social heritage). In a predominantly heterosexual society this tends to be towards the generally accepted family lifestyle, of which marriage is an integral part. If it is the case

1

that married homosexual men marry as a result of social pressures, then it seems a reasonable proposition that such people may be a good example of homosexual men over-responding to social pressure. As a consequence, the investigation of the married homosexual man may well have utility not only from the point of view of casting light on a specific issue, but also from the point of view of looking at the general mechanisms by which homosexuals (or any other stigmatised minority) internalise, and act upon, social pressures.

Gagnon and Simon (1973) have pointed out that: 'We have allowed the homosexual's object choice to dominate and control our imagery of him.' Going further, Evans (1974) has suggested that: 'the importance of the homosexuality itself in the adjustment of the homosexual (is) over-emphasised. . . . the only meaningful difference between homosexuals and heterosexuals is their sexual preference.' While the psychological literature on homosexuality tends to support the idea that a person's object choice as such has no implications for other psychological characteristics, the presence of 'unconventional sexuality' (homosexuality) in a person can lead to social pressure on that individual. In turn, this may produce the problems of adjustment which some homosexuals show, whether they are a result of immediate social situations or social influences on personality.

In the married homosexual, there is a double difficulty in adjustment, resulting also from the need to adjust to one's sexual preference within the context of a relationship which is usually for an explicitly contrary sexual preference. Thus, since social pressure appears to be a major contributor to any differences which may be found between some homosexuals and heterosexuals, the study of married homosexual males could well give an insight into the mechanisms of adjustment difficulties based on social pressure in many of those homosexuals who present for assistance, whether married or not.

Weinberg and Williams (1974) studied male homosexuals in three cultures in which there were different degrees of social pressure against homosexuality, and predicted that the psychological well-being and relating to homosexual and heterosexual worlds of the respondents would reflect the social climate of their culture. No such significant differences were found. However, it is suggested that to the homosexual the critical aspect of social pressure is not the overall societal reaction, but the *perceived* societal reaction, the way the individual sees and reacts to the social pressure. If the proposition that married homosexual men are reacting to social pressure to conform is correct, then this group should show less psychological well-being than a control group of unmarried homosexual men. The married homosexual man, in comparison with the non-married homosexual, is seen thus as one who sees social pressure against homosexuality and towards the family life-style and marriage as being stronger or more important than his own sexual preference.

There is considerable evidence (H. L. Ross, 1971) to suggest that the married homosexual man is in a situation of some conflict. Do such difficulties in marriage arise out of the marriage situation itself or the psychological characteristics of the marrying homosexual? The possibility is that the marriage of the homosexual is either personality-determined, in terms of there being a particular type of homosexual who will react to societal pressure against his sexual preference by marrying, and thus be at risk prior to marriage; or situational, in the sense that it is the problems of the double-life in marriage which creates conflict. On the other hand, it may be that very little conflict is generated: an adequate empirical investigation needs to be made of the whole area.

The concepts of 'psychological adjustment' and 'situational factors' will be defined in terms of specific items and scales in the questionnaire administered to the sample. Sampling, of course, constitutes a central problem in any study on homosexuality. Weinberg (1970) states that it is impossible to obtain a representative homosexual sample. Most studies to date have used samples from the 'Gay subculture', in which there is considerable bias towards acculturation, some degree of overtness, and a higher educational and socio-economic level. While the present sample can be no more representative than others, the purpose of this study is the examination of a sub-group in the homosexual world, the consideration of the parameters of the social problem of the married homosexual man, and the testing of hypotheses in the areas of societal reaction theory and psychological characteristics of socially pressured homosexuals.

The study covers three main areas: first, the production of a socio-psychological profile of the married homosexual male; second, a study of the forms of adaptation of homosexual men who have married; and third, an investigation of the role of putative societal reaction in yielding to social influence, and a subsidiary investigation of a number of hypotheses on the nature of social pressure and its effects on the homosexual sub-group. These hypotheses will be spelled out in detail in the appropriate chapters. In general, though, it can be said that the questions as to why homosexual men marry, how they cope, and how the lay person and professional alike may better understand the phenomenon in order to deal with it, are the central issues to be addressed.

2 Existing research on the married homosexual man

Any relevant research literature on the married homosexual man falls into two categories: those studies which look at broader aspects of homosexuality, and incidentally provide information on the proportion of homosexuals who have married; and those which look at several cases in some depth. The former tend to be epidemiological, reporting useful statistics on prevalence and incidence, but not going any deeper into the phenomenon. The latter tend to be case-histories, usually of ten cases or less, which may not be particularly representative of married homosexual men and which tend to emphasise those who have problems. In general, the findings of those studies which look at prevalence are fairly similar across Western cultures, and their data can be assumed to be accurate, despite the fact that they are over-representative of the middle-class, educated individuals who are usually sampled through Gay organisations and public venues such as bars and social clubs. This problem of representativeness of sampling will be dealt with in greater detail later.

The earliest formal research which cast any light on the issue of male homosexuality, and parenthetically on the prevalence of married homosexuals, was the famous Kinsey Report of the late 1940s (Kinsey, Pomeroy and Martin, 1948). Kinsey *et al.*'s study is too well known to require any more than a brief description. The data, which included in-depth interviews with over five thousand three hundred white American men, collected between 1938 and 1947, caused a sensation on publication because of the evidence that homosexual behaviour was relatively common in the population, and because it became clear that people were not 'homosexual' or 'heterosexual', but were placed on a continuum. This so-called Kinsey Scale is composed of seven positions, graded from 0-6. Individuals classified as 0 are described as heterosexual: they make no physical contacts which result in erotic arousal or orgasm with members of their own sex. Those rated 1 have had only incidental homosexual contact, and the great preponderence of their social-sexual experience is with females. Position 2 individuals will have more than incidental homosexual experience, but it is surpassed by the amount of heterosexual experience they may have in a similar time span. Individuals rated 3 are probably closest to what is commonly called bisexual: they have roughly equal amounts of homosexual and heterosexual behaviour and/or are attracted equally to males and females. On the other side of the Kinsey Scale, the individuals rated 4 have more than incidental heterosexual experience but with homosexuality predominating: the individual rated 5 will have incidental heterosexual experience but be predominantly homosexual. The individual rated 6 is the homosexual equivalent of 0, where the sexual preference is totally toward other men. While Kinsey *et al.* noted that some 37 per cent of the male population (over one-third) had had at least one overt homosexual experience leading to orgasm between the ages of 15 and 55, when the married homosexual man is referred to, it is the individual who has a rating of 3 or higher who is the subject of this study. In addition, those referred to in subsequent research as well as the present study have also identified themselves as homosexual.

Kinsey *et al.*'s work, however, while including a breakdown of their data, do not label the individuals beyond their position on the Kinsey Scale. They also analyse their data in terms of the educational level of their subjects, which provides some interesting insights: in order to better appreciate the way Kinsey *et al.* have reported their information, a breakdown of one of their summary tables appears in Table 2.1.

Kinsey *et al.*'s data are of particular interest because unlike the data of other studies, which give us the proportions of homosexual men who have married, these data give us the

Table 2.1 **Heterosexual-homosexual rating, cumulative incidence in married males, lower educational levels**

				Kinsey Scale level, %			
Age	n	0	1+	2+	3+	4+	5+
20	134	90.3	9.7	7.5	4.5	0	0
25	238	92.0	8.0	6.3	2.1	0.4	0
30	207	94.7	5.3	3.9	1.0	0	0
35	162	95.7	4.3	3.7	0	0	0
40	125	92.8	6.4	4.8	0.8	0.8	0
45	75	96.1	2.6	1.3	0	0	0

Adapted from Table 148, Kinsey, A.C., Pomeroy, W. B., and Martin, C. E., *Sexual Behaviour in the Human Male*, Philadelphia: W. B. Saunders, 1948.

proportion of married men who are homosexual. This also enables a check of one set of figures against the other.

From Table 2.1, it can be seen that, for the age groups 20-24 to 45-49 of married men, an average of 1.7 per cent of the primary school graduates, and 1.9 per cent of the college graduates, were at level 3 on the Kinsey scale. In effect, given that this indicates that their homosexual experience was at least equal to their heterosexual experience: given that they were married, and had permanent access to heterosexual sex, their homosexual sexual experience must have been considerable. It is of interest that the highest figure (4.5 per cent) is for the lower education group, and tends to decline after the age group 20-24; for the college-educated group, however, it tends to increase above the less educated group from the age group 25-29. What this suggests is that there are two different circumstances of married homosexual men, which to some degree depend on educational level, and, therefore, socio-economic status. With the lower-educated, lower socio-economic status group the homosexual activity appears to peak in the late teens-early twenties, and decline following this period. This could well represent hustling or the opportunity for frequent and possibly relatively impersonal sex while the individual is young and attractive. On the other hand, the increase above the lower-educated group by those who have a higher educational level, and thus higher socio-economic status, from the 25-29 age group, suggests that homosexual activity is something which occurs much later, presumably as a function of an awareness of the individual's homosexual sexual preference slowly developing. This conception of the two groups of married homosexual men fits in well with data of Humphreys (1970), reviewed below.

At this point, however, it is necessary to look at several theoretical issues which are helpful in examining the position of the married homosexual.

Dickey (1961) has noted that the subjectively adequate homosexual man tends to identify with the dominant masculine norms. Dominant masculine norms, however, include marriage (although to a lesser degree now than previously). In this regard, classical theory of the psychoanalytic school is worthy of noting. Adler suggests that one form of overcompensation in men may take the form of a 'masculine protest', in which homosexual or feminine traits are hidden by hypertrophied, overexaggerated masculine wishes or efforts. Marriage may be one form of this overreaction to homosexuality or femininity. However, where this 'masculine protest' succeeds, for example when a homosexual marries or a feminine individual takes up a supermasculine pursuit, the masculine tendencies are strengthened to such an extent that restlessness and resentment occur with the homosexual or feminine traits still present and pressing for expression. In this sort of situation, conflicts may often occur.

Similarly, Jung suggests that every individual possesses both masculine and feminine personality traits (animus and anima, meaning male spirit and female spirit). The individual will put on a mask (the 'persona'), which corresponds with the conscious intentions, requirements and opinions of his environment. In the case of the homosexual, this may well be reflected in the 'anima', or the homosexual identity, being hidden behind an 'animus'-dominated persona of masculine traits, which include marriage and other socially expected behaviours consistent with such a role. However, the question is still raised as to whether any conflicts in the marriage situation for homosexual men are a result of the marriage situation, or the identification with and excessive conformity to the dominant norms of society, or both.

In practical terms, the gap between theory and practice may also be bridged by a study which also covers the grey area between the study by Kinsey *et al.*, which looked at the proportion of married men who engaged in homosexual activity, and research which looks at the proportion of the homosexual population which has married. Humphreys (1970) studied homosexual activities in public conveniences ('Tearooms' in American slang, hence the title of his book, *Tearoom Trade*). His method was extremely innovative, and bears some explanation. While the main purpose of the study was to deal with stigmatised behaviour in terms of how it was organised and the rules for interaction within the public convenience, Humphreys also took the license-plate numbers of the cars in which men came to the conveniences. From local records, he was able to obtain names and addresses, as well as marital and occupational status for the participants. Some fifty of the hundred license-plate numbers obtained led to in-depth interviews with the men who had been observed having sex with other men in a public convenience, with Humphreys posing as a market researcher in order to interview them in their homes.

Over half (54 per cent) were married and living with their wives. There was no evidence that these marriages were any more unstable than other marriages, nor that the wives were aware of their husband's secret sexual activity: in fact, Humphreys suggests that the public convenience was chosen for just this reason. In most cases, it was apparent that the respondent's desire for sex that was fast, impersonal, and did not lead to any identifying details being given was primarily to protect their families. However, when the interview schedules were analysed, a pattern emerged which was referred to as 'conjugal role separation', in which the predominant pattern of married life involved separate and different activities of husband and wife, but activities which fitted together to form a functioning unit. Thus the marriage tended to be composed of separate but interlocking activities of husband and wife with a minimum of interaction. Some eleven (41 per cent) of the homosexually active men's marriages were of this sort, compared with only three of the couples in the heterosexual control sample: it does suggest that this sort of compartmentalisation may be one response to the situation of marriage in homosexual men.

The married men in Humphrey's sample could be divided into two groups in terms of their education and occupation: this division offers a classification which is remarkably similar to the education level classification of Kinsey *et al.* in 1948. The first classification ('Trade', according to Humphreys), comprised 38 per cent of the homosexually active group, and all were, or had been, married. Most worked as truck drivers, machine operators, or clerical workers: one in six was black. Particularly telling is the overrepresentation of Roman Catholics: in 63 per cent of marriages, husband, wife or both are Catholic. More will be made of this when reasons for marriage are considered in Chapter 5. Truck drivers were the biggest single occupational group in the 'Trade' category; their median age was 38, with an average of 2.2 children. The group was called 'Trade' because two-thirds took the active (insertor) role in the fellatio in public conveniences, and because they would be classified in the homosexual subculture as such: men who do not consider themselves homosexual (or will not admit to it), as long as they do not take a passive role. Humphreys considers that there is no indication that these men seek homosexual contact as such; rather, they want a form of orgasm-producing action less lonely than masturbation and less involving than a love relationship. On the other hand, one could argue that since one-third did perform in the passive (insertee) role, and since the act of fellatio was performed almost invariably in silence and in the shortest time possible, it was so akin to masturbation that there must have been good reason to choose a male partner rather than to masturbate. Certainly in terms of sex of partner, these men who Humphreys calls 'Trade' were homosexual. Length and degree of intimacy in any encounter are not what gives rise to the classification of homosexual or heterosexual: as Stern and Stern (1981) report similar heterosexual encounters on buses in Russia,

it would seem unjustified not to classify them as heterosexual simply because they were anonymous and brief.
The essence of the encounters Humphreys describes in the
'Trade' group is perhaps denial of homosexuality rather
than anything else: denial by the participant as well as
to his family, friends or even to other homosexuals.

The second classificatory group Humphreys describes are
the ambisexuals. These married men have double the median
income of the 'Trade' group, 1.6 children on average, a median age of 43, and are usually Protestants. In terms of their
observed role in fellatio, two-thirds were insertees, one-third
insertors. Ambisexuals are much more likely to be middle
class or upper-middle class, and to be more open about their
homosexual preferences. Humphreys also noted that nearly
two-thirds of the ambisexuals were college graduates, which
tends to put them into the group of Kinsey *et al.* which included those with tertiary education. However, by openness
about their homosexual preference, is meant to other homosexuals. In all the cases which are cited by Humphreys none
of the spouses or heterosexual friends knew. Such ambisexuals are not fleeing from unhappy home lives or sexless
marriages, but usually express great devotion to their wives
and families. The pattern for their sexual preferences was
almost one of separation and compartmentalisation: as
Humphreys cites one of his ambisexual subjects, 'You might
think I live two lives, but if I do, I don't feel split in two by
them.' Such individuals recognised their homosexual activity as part of their psychosexual orientation, and themselves as bisexual (which behaviourally they are). Contacts
with other homosexuals (although not usually individuals
from the more public homosexual subculture such as bars
and clubs) are common, as is reading about homosexuality.
These ambisexual individuals appear to cope because they
do seem to have a significant degree of heterosexual responsiveness as well as homosexual preference, and thus the
heterosexual marriage has rewarding aspects. The more the
individual is homosexual in preference (that is, the closer he
is to position 6 on the Kinsey scale), however, the more
likely there will be pressure on the marriage and towards a
homosexual emotional, as well as sexual, relationship.

Perhaps the most startling aspect of Humphrey's study concerns what he calls the 'breast plate of righteousness', or 'refulgent respectability'. By this, he refers to the cloud of propriety and respectability which surrounds the married homosexual. He suggests that the 'covert deviant' develops a self-presentation that is overly respectable and orthodox: this includes often a highly conservative political and social stance. As with the actual marriage of homosexual man, this may again be seen in the light of overcompensation in one direction to hide the unconventional sexual orientation. The rationale is probably something alone the lines of 'if I express the view that civil rights for homosexuals are necessary, people may start to suspect I'm one.' This, however, goes much further than issues with regard to sexuality: Humphreys found that on indices of liberalism relating to economic reform, the civil rights movement, the Vietnam war, and police practices, the married homosexuals, particularly the 'Trade' group, were much more conservative than a matched control group. Even more surprising was the fact that those in the lower and lower-middle class encouraged more vice-squad activity, and some could even be described as moral crusaders: several were also members of the John Birch Society, an ultra right-wing American organisation!

These data underscore an important theoretical point with regard to married homosexual men. It becomes clear that overcompensation is occurring in an attempt to deny their homosexual orientation, to the extent that it could be described as reaction formation. Reaction formation refers to a psychological defence mechanism in which the individual reacts to an event or state by moving to the extreme opposite state in terms of attitude or behaviour. That this occurs with socio-political attitudes in some married homosexuals does suggest another theoretical base for marriage. It could be postulated that those who are homosexual to some degree and who marry are not just reacting to their homosexuality by covering up with the 'breast plate of righteousness', but that they were even prior to marriage conservative, and that their marriage was just one manifestation of this. The question is thus repeated: is this a *function* of marriage, or a *reason* for it?

In looking at data from studies which examine the married homosexual man within the context of the homosexual subculture, it is probable that only the more overt or well-adjusted married homosexuals have been sampled, and this bias must be taken into account when making conclusions. It is debatable whether any sample of homosexuals is representative, and any 'tip of the iceberg' sample is likely to be even less so. Nevertheless, such selective research does produce a greater depth of information compared with the epidemiological survey. Perhaps the classic early study on the married homosexual man was that of H. L. Ross (1971).

Ross studied the situations and modes of adjustment of eleven married homosexuals in Belgium. While noting that the married homosexual was an important but rather obscure social problem, and that no firm conclusions could be reached because of the small number and case-history method, Ross noted that subjects fell into two groups, those who discovered their homosexuality after marriage and subsequently redefined their status after a homosexual affair, and those who knew of their homosexuality prior to marriage, and who were possibly in a conscious flight from their homosexuality. Some of this latter group felt their orientation was situational and would disappear with marriage. In general, both groups had little sexual experience of any sort before marriage. The marriage had been a result of a number of factors, including advice from a doctor or priest, a rational choice because of the subject's family-centred values, social pressures from family and relatives, work and loneliness. Weinberg (1970) has noted that loneliness amongst homosexuals is most common in those under 25.

Several main sources of conflict within the marriage were also noted by Ross. Sexual problems tended to increase as the marriage continued: when the partners found out the husband was homosexual they felt defrauded and resentful, and any deep homosexual relationships on the part of the subjects were resented, while jealousy also occurred in some cases. However, the establishment of a homosexual liaison was often the greatest compensation for marital problems and sometimes, surprisingly, kept the marriage together. All the married subjects took part in the local 'Gay Life', but their spouses were suspicious and recriminating.

Four main modes of adjustment were noted among the subjects: first was separation, if there were no children of the marriage and no 'satisfactions' of married life. Such satisfactions would include non-sexual and non-affective ones, such as common home, division of labour, companionship and social respectability. Fear of subject's inability to lead a separate and independent life, and an adjustment to the psychological peculiarities of the partner were also factors which led to separation. Second, there was the 'platonic' marriage, which involved abandoning the sexual side of the marriage and concentrating on other marital satisfactions and outside interests, such as job, children, etc. Any sexual contacts occurred outside the marriage. Third, the 'double-standard' marriage, which involved an outside homosexual liaison as well as marriage, occurred. This was probably the hoped-for ideal of the second type, 'platonic' marriage. However, it was resented by the spouse, who felt a dual commitment was unable to be maintained. Fourth, the 'innovative' marriage, characterised by frequent heterosexual relations as well as homosexual relations, all quite openly, was seen as a possible solution. In one case, a 'ménage à trois' occurred. In this type of marriage, true bisexuality rather than homosexuality could be said to be a contributing factor to the adjustment.

The effectiveness of these adjustments, Ross felt, was variable. All adjustments occurred in the context of apparent near-complete acceptance of conventional norms by most of the subjects. Thus they were rather poor solutions to conflict between heterosexuality and homosexuality. The 'platonic' marriage engendered mutual dissatisfaction and a displacement from the marital tie. Biological and psychological frustration was the result, often overtly expressed and with mutual guilt. Devaluation of the spouse led to bitterness and aggression toward the husband. 'Innovative' marriage appeared the most successful and free from interpersonal conflicts, but this depended on the versatility of the husband and the broad-mindedness of the wife.

While the work of Ross contributes a great deal to the preliminary analysis of the situation of married homosexuals, it raises a number of points from which some testable hypotheses can be generated. These need to be followed up with a larger and hopefully more representative sample: although as previously noted, a truly 'representative' sample of homosexuals is impossible to obtain a broader range is a possibility as a result of a larger number.

Saghir and Robins (1973), in a comprehensive investigation of homosexuality, observed not only some aspects of the adaptations and factors affecting married homosexuals, but also those affecting homosexuals generally. While Saghir and Robins used a matched sample of 124 men (89 homosexuals and 35 heterosexuals), a problem which occurred was retrospective distortion. This occurred as a function of hindsight and rationalisation. This problem is a common one, and almost impossible to control for: M. W. Ross (1980) noted it could occur in three ways. First, faulty recall; second, intentional falsified reporting; and third, knowledge about the commonly held antecedents of a homosexual orientation. It is this last category which could conceivably bias recall, with individuals reporting common conceptions or misconceptions about married homosexuals.

However, results of this investigation showed some interesting facts. 59 per cent of the homosexuals sampled showed, or had had, some romantic attachment of a heterosexual nature during their life. 48 per cent had had sexual relations with a woman. Data on stable heterosexual relationships continue these figures: 53 per cent of the homosexuals had had one or more stable heterosexual relationship, either marital or non-marital, over a period of a year. On the basis of these data, it could be implied that a fair proportion of homosexuals could be in a situation in which marriage could occur. Of the total sample, 18 per cent had been married. Broken down, these figures are produced: 12 per cent married and divorced, 3 per cent married and separated, 2 per cent still married, 1 per cent widowed. That nearly a fifth of this sample have been married suggests that the situation is not uncommon, even in such a relatively 'overt' sample. Age at marriage was found to be under 25 (60 per cent), 25-29 (13 per cent) and over 30 (27 per cent). That the majority marry under 25 could well be connected with the finding of Weinberg (1970) that most loneliness in homosexuals occurs in this period. It could be suggested that for these under 25, marriage is an attempt at heterosexual adjustment when conflict about homosexuality is at its peak, or a result of family and social pressure.

Of those who married, and then separated or divorced, 70 per cent had lived with their wives less than three years, 30 per cent more than three years. Reasons for the break-up are very similar to those found by H. L. Ross (1971), most being because of emotional and sexual dissatisfaction. While 76 per cent of the homosexual sample described their wives as aggressive and unsympathetic, 75 per cent of the heterosexual control sample describe their spouses as the same. Nevertheless, homosexuals who married often stated that the marriage was initiated by the wife.

Reasons for marriage were also similar to those found by Ross: 94 per cent of the married sample gave the reason for marriage as social acceptance, family or girlfriend pressure, and domestic needs or a desire for children. 79 per cent of the previously married homosexuals said they would not marry again, as did 71 per cent of the unmarried homosexuals. Two of the total sample were still living with their wives. Both were leading successful homosexual and heterosexual lives without threat to the marriage and neither of the wives knew. In each case the subject preferred homosexual relations, although both types of relations were satisfying both emotionally and physically. Heterosexual relations were monogamous, homosexual relatively promiscuous. Only one subject was married to a lesbian, and the marriage broke up as a result of jealousy (on the part of the man).

Most of Saghir and Robins's subjects (62 per cent) had desired a change in their orientation at some time in their life, and of these, 67 per cent desired it before the age of 25. And again, of these 62 per cent, 45 per cent (that is, 31 per cent of the total sample) sought to de-emphasise their homosexuality by becoming involved heterosexually.

These data amply demonstrate that a high proportion of homosexuals become heterosexually involved as an attempted compensation for their homosexuality, usually before the age of 25. At the other end of the scale, some 28 per cent of the subjects feared growing old and being lonely. It is possible that some later marriages may stem from this factor.

Confirmation of these findings is provided to a large extent by Weinberg and Williams (1974), who, using a large number of 2,437 homosexuals in the US, Denmark and the Netherlands, examined the adjustment and adaptation of these subjects in the light of societal reaction theory.

Societal reaction theory would expect married homosexuals to be less well adjusted than their unmarried peers, not only as a result of conflict between their orientation and existing situation, but also because of their different way of relating to the heterosexual world and a higher exposure to traditional values, which, in Western society, are anti-homosexual. Thus married homosexuals would be expected to be the most secretive of the sample, first to prevent the spouse's discovery and second because of their greater acceptance of current standards. Further, psychological problems of homosexuals tend to be greater without the support of others with the same status, and Weinberg and Williams have noted a bimodal distribution of relating to the homosexual subculture. That is, there are two groups in terms of relating to the 'Gay scene': one bunched up at the top end of the scale who are strongly involved, and the other at the bottom end who have no, or almost no, contact with the homosexual subculture. It can be suggested that many married homosexuals would be in the lower relationship portion of the distribution.

The study also notes 17 per cent of those sampled have been married, a proportion which agrees well with the findings of Saghir and Robins (1973). Of these, 49 per cent of the wives knew their husbands were homosexual, 16 per cent may have known, and 34 per cent did not know. Such a high proportion of wives cognisant of their husband's status is probably a reflection of the nature of the sample, which is biased toward those who take part in the homosexual

17

subculture. Subjects in the subculture are more likely to be overt, and to have the necessary support to be able to 'come out'. Of those subjects married, the projected reactions of the spouse were 57 per cent accepting to tolerant, 43 per cent intolerant to rejecting. A tendency in the general sample, with education controlled for, was for the younger homosexual to be less well adjusted. Again this supports earlier findings.

A number of interesting findings which will be used to generate hypotheses with regard to married homosexuals, but which, in the work of Weinberg and Williams occur as factors in the adaptation of single homosexuals, will be discussed briefly here. They noted that the higher the level of adjustment, the lower the femininity of the subject, which confirms subjective findings of Hooker (1965) and others. A high commitment to homosexuality as a way of life was found to be correlated with higher psychological well-being and also with acceptance of homosexuality as normal. Infrequent (homosexual) sex, loneliness and never having had an exclusive (homosexual) relationship, correlated highly with a lack of psychological well-being. Worry about exposure of one's homosexuality and passing as a heterosexual (referred to as 'passing' below, were compared, and it was noted that it was the worry about exposure rather than the passing as such which led to a higher proportion of psychological problems. It was consequently suggested that 'compartmentalisation' of interests and activities plays a large part in the adaptation of homosexuals to societal reactions. A further finding of interest was that those with low involvement in the homosexual subculture felt more threatened by the heterosexual world. It was suggested that greater involvement would mean more support and less threat. No great problems were noted for those who were bisexual (*not* married), however. Those subjects living at home had a chronic fear of exposure.

Some specific factors were noted about those subjects who were, at the time of the study, living with their wives. These homosexuals were most likely to worry about exposure, at least known about by other homosexuals, highest in passing as a heterosexual, bisexual, less likely to be involved with other homosexuals and less involved in the subculture, and had fewer close friends over two years. Weinberg and Williams suggest that married homosexuals obtain from their families and other heterosexuals the gratifications that other homosexuals with other living arrangements obtain from the homosexual world. In effect, the suggestion is that compartmentalisation occurs in terms of sexual preference, and that gratification need not necessarily be associated with any particular source, male or female. While married homosexuals tend to show considerable amounts of guilt, shame and anxiety over their homosexuality, they appear to be within the normal range with regard to their other subscales measuring psychological adjustment. All these findings were controlled for level of social involvement. Weinberg and Williams find that, in general, their data are not as expected in terms of the societal reaction so much as how the individual reacts to that societal reaction; in other words, the *individual* holds the clues to the situation.

Societal reaction theory holds that homosexuals in more anti-homosexual societies will have worse psychological adjustment, in particular be less self-accepting, have less self-esteem, and feel more badly about homosexuality, than those in more accepting societies. However, Weinberg and Williams found this was not the case in the three societies they looked at (the United States, Denmark and the Netherlands). Following this, M. W. Ross (1978) suggested that the critical variable was not the *actual* societal reaction, but the way the homosexuals *perceived* it. It subsequently turned out that perceived societal reaction did predict a significantly lowered state of psychological well-being, although actual societal reaction did not.

Degree of homosexuality is also an important variable which may have some bearing on marital adjustment. Imieliński (1969) studied the correlation between the degree of homosexuality in male homosexuals, and success of marriage. However, all twenty-eight subjects were clinical cases or prison-referred. Degree of homosexuality was measured on a modified Kinsey Scale, and it was found that only those subjects with degree 1 and most with degree 2 homosexuality had successful marriages: from degree 3 on the success of marriage declined dramatically. Reasons for marriage in order of importance were (1) physician's advice; (2) desire for children; (3) emotional relationships with women; (4) need for somebody to keep house. No doubt this study reflects the greater condemnation of homosexuality in Eastern Europe (Warsaw) in 1969. Nevertheless, the point is made that the higher the degree of homosexuality, the less chance any marriage has of surviving.

Data similar to that found by H. L. Ross (1971) and Saghir and Robins (1973) is provided by the study of Dannecker and Reiche (1974) in the Federal Republic of (West) Germany. Dannecker and Reiche found that, of their sample of 789 homosexual males, 10 per cent had been married or were still married (5 per cent of each). It was suggested that the 1:1 relationship of existing to broken marriages showed that adaptation was not very successful, or that not many homosexual men had found what they were looking for in marriage. For some two-thirds, the spouse did not know of the husband's homosexuality at the time of marriage, and of these, half never knew. Such an arrangement, and its correlated purpose of using marriage as a means of hiding homosexuality, caused marriage of homosexuals to be labelled a 'collective neurosis' by the authors. Reasons for marriage were varied: the three most important were (1) to have a lifelong companion; (2) to have children; (3) to hide one's homosexuality. 56 per cent of married subjects ticked at least one statement which mentioned resistance to, or hiding of, homosexuality. Those who also said they married with the desire for 'sexual intercourse with a woman' tended to rate their marriage as not very happy, perhaps indicating the sexual or role conflict met within the situation.

Subjects were further analysed by degree of homosexual sexual activity. Those who had low homosexual activity also had low sexual activity with their wives, and those who showed a high degree of homosexual activity also had a high level of sex with their wives. An interesting corollary was that those subjects who regarded their marriage as happy had a higher degree of homosexual sex than those who regarded their marriage as not so happy. Married subjects did not differ appreciably from non-married homosexuals: age of coming out as a homosexual was similar, all knew they were homosexuals before marriage, and no greater proportion wished to be 'treated' nor disliked homosexual activities. Average age at time of marriage was 27. A certain degree of role-conflict was noted and discussed. Homosexuals in society, without particular help, were, it was felt, socialised into the institution of monogamous marriage. The decision to marry would appear to be a 'sub-conscious social process', forceful but beyond control, evidenced only as a 'conformity' to the family life-style. So the contradictions of heterosexual norm and homosexual 'abnormality' exist in each homosexual who has married, they claim.

Bisexuality was not seen as a problem either in theory or practice. Many subjects in Dannecker and Reiche's total sample (56 per cent) had had sexual intercourse with women. This does not imply bisexuality, since many tried to overcompensate their homosexuality through excessive heterosexuality, or because of wavering between hetero- and homosexuality, afraid of being recognised as a homosexual. Many case studies showed that it is useless, in a society in which heterosexuality is the favoured norm, to derive the 'bisexuality' of a person from the amount of his homo- or heterosexual activity. It was suggested that all bisexuals are really predominantly homosexuals: some such people were referred to as 'defence-bisexuals'. However, while it is stressed by Dannecker and Reiche that married homosexuals were not a special group in many respects, they pointed out the importance of 'illuminating and empirically working out the marriage motive'. (p. 367): it was not believed that marriage was solely a defence mechanism against homosexuality, but that more important objective or subjective reasons existed. It was to provide that illumination and empirical evidence that the study reported in this book was conducted.

There is one subsequent study from the Kinsey Institute at Indiana University which has looked at epidemiological considerations in regard to married homosexuals. As part of a larger study of male and female homosexualities, Bell and Weinberg (1978) obtained a sample of homosexual men, both white and black, in San Francisco in the early 1970s. Sources of recruitment included public advertising, personal contacts, bars, public baths, homophile organisations, and public places: in this way, interviews could finally be conducted with 3,854 homosexual men (3,538 white, 316 black). They noted that while marriage was not commonplace, nor was it unusual: however, they also noted that it was usually unhappy and short-lived, and that almost all ended in separation or divorce. White homosexual men had a marriage rate of 20 per cent, blacks 13 per cent: average age of marriage was at 24. The fact that most marriages were short-lived and usually ended in separation or divorce is most probably a reflection of the nature of the sample, which was heavily weighted towards the more overt and better educated individual. The additional fact that the sample was predominantly from San Francisco, held by some to be the largest 'Gay city' in the world, suggests a bias toward overt and better-adjusted homosexuals. It is perhaps significant that even in this sort of sample within this sort of environment, one fifth had been married. This proportion is also roughly similar to that found by Saghir and Robins (1973) and Weinberg and Williams (1974).

An interesting finding by Bell and Weinberg was that those homosexuals who in later (homosexual) relationships were what they called close coupled and open coupled (that is, in monogamous and exogamous relationships respectively) had married significantly younger than other groups. There is a hint in this that those who married younger may have done so because of their need or desire for a relationship and a need for affection and the stability of a partner. Bell and Weinberg also report that the homosexuals felt their marriages to be less happy than those of the heterosexual controls. This contrasts with the finding of Saghir and Robins that there was equal marriage dissatisfaction, and suggests that there may be some degree of rationalisation in those who report an unhappy marriage. For example, they may justify their move to a solely homosexual sex object preference and separation from their wife by saying that 'it wasn't really happy anyway'. On the other hand, the heterosexual control group were more sexually active in both the first and last years of marriage, which does tend to suggest that heterosexual sex was less important for the married homosexuals, and for this reason, the marriages may well have been less happy. In addition, the Bell and Weinberg sample were predominantly points 5 and 6 on the Kinsey Scale: one-third of the white and one-fifth of the black married homosexuals fantasised that they were having sex with men while having sex with their wives often; nearly half (40 per cent) did so occasionally. More than a third had in fact told their wives of their sexual orientation prior to marriage (although not that they would do anything about it). Nearly half were married for about three years or longer (one quarter for only 1-2 years, one quarter for 11 years or longer). In over half the white (54 per cent) and less than a quarter of the black (23 per cent) married homosexuals, their homosexuality had something to do with the ending of the marriage. In particular, factors such as becoming involved with another male (48 per cent), lack of interest in heterosexual sex (20 per cent), the spouse finding out her husband was homosexual (18 per cent), and being unable to sexually satisfy the spouse were mentioned. Half the white men had no children of the marriage, while half the black men had had one child.

With regard to being aware of their homosexuality prior to marriage, only 15 per cent of the white men and none of the black men had not been aware they were homosexual prior to marriage: this strongly suggests that social or societal factors may have played a major part in the decision to wed.

Corroborating evidence comes from a study by Masters and Johnson (1979), who found that of their homosexual male sample, 17 per cent had been married previously: these marriages had lasted periods from one week to seventeen years! Of the bisexuals that Masters and Johnson studied, none had married. Further, nearly two-thirds of their homosexual men who had married (61 per cent) had done so in an attempt to reverse their homosexual preference. This accords quite well with the reasons which Bell and Weinberg's sample report for marriage: attempting to hide one's sexual orientation, to test their heterosexual responsiveness, deny their homosexuality, accommodate to social pressures, disappointment with homosexual lovers (all negatively related to homosexuality). Other reasons given were more positive, including flight from an intolerable parental relationship, a desire for a stable and permanent relationship, affection for spouse, and a desire for children.

It can thus be seen that in terms of the epidemiology of marriage in homosexuals, all the studies to date which have touched on the area produce substantially similar figures in different samples and in different Western societies. There is corroboration of the 1.7-1.9 per cent which Kinsey *et al.* reported in 1948 from a Dutch study (Noordhoff, 1970), which indicated that 1.3 per cent of married Dutch males were homosexual: this is all the more impressive given the discrepancies in time and culture. Similarly, the figures of between 10 per cent and 20 per cent who had been married in the studies of homosexuals carried out in the United States, the Netherlands, Denmark, and West Germany are in substantial agreement. Again, some incidental corroboration of this is provided by Lautmann (1980-1), reporting on the persecution of homosexual males in concentration camps in Nazi Germany between 1933 and 1945. Lautmann notes in passing that of the data on some 700 homosexuals to which he had access, 16 per cent had been married or widowed. Such indirect evidence strongly suggests that the proportions reported here are reliable and may reflect accurately the magnitude of the phenomenon in Western societies. From the evidence of reasons for marriage, the data available also suggest a strong social or societal component in the decision to marry. It is therefore necessary to follow through and to look in some detail at the marriage situation of married homosexuals and how this may be affected by the reasons for marriage, and the adjustments to marriage.

3 Marriages of homosexuals: reasons, coping and consequences

Reasons advanced already for marriage among homosexuals are many and varied, but can be placed for convenience into five categories. First, social pressure from an external source such as family, friends, or particularly from the girlfriend. Second, as an explicit attempt to remove or de-emphasise one's homosexuality, or because it was regarded as a passing phase which would disappear. Third, because the man was genuinely in love with his partner and wanted to live with her, and possibly from a desire for married life and children. Fourth, because the individual was unaware of his homosexuality at the time of his marriage, or was unable to label his feelings of being 'different', and finally, and often in older homosexual men, for companionship. Obviously there are other reasons which may emerge which do not fit neatly into these categories, and equally obviously, the decision to marry may often be a mixture of reasons across different categories. Evidence for and examples of, these reasons are sprinkled throughout the scientific literature: unfortunately, because of the fact that many reports are based on a few case studies or biased samples, it is difficult if not impossible to guess just how common these reasons are.

Social pressure from external sources, either direct or indirect, has been put forward many times as an explanation for marriage of homosexuals. The Report of the Committee on Homosexual Offences and Prostitution in Great Britain (The Wolfenden Report, 1957) pointed out that:

25

it has to be recognised that the mere existence of the condition of homosexuality in one of the partners can result in an unsatisfactory marriage, so that for a homosexual to marry simply for the sake of conformity with the accepted structure of society or in the hope of curing his condition may result in disaster.

In most of the reasons given for homosexual men marrying, social pressures of varying degrees are listed. H. L. Ross (1971) points out that, in the ten men he interviewed, four reasons emerged for marriage (in no particular order, and not necessarily being mutually exclusive of one another). First, that the individuals didn't know they were homosexual, although they knew they were 'different'. Such people usually had had a predominance of same-sex relationships but considered themselves heterosexual, until they redefined themselves after a homosexual love affair. It is particularly interesting that Ross interviewed his sample in Belgium in 1970, at a time and in a country where homosexuality, and sexual topics generally, were not discussed. Probably as homosexuality becomes a more open subject of discussion, this reason may become less common.

The second reason noted by Ross was conscious flight from homosexuality. Again, in a society and at a time where homosexuality was not discussed, or only referred to in the most negative terms, this may have been more common than now. Most of the men he interviewed felt that their homosexuality was situational, and would disappear in marriage. They usually had had little if any sex prior to marriage, and came from moralistic, puritanical families. Often, Ross notes, the advice to marry would come from a priest or chaplain. The point can be made at many stages in research on married homosexuals, that in societies where there is no education, or negative education, regarding homosexuality, there will most likely be a greater number of homosexuals who lead unhappy lives and lack self-esteem. There will also be a greater number who marry, either in ignorance of their sexual orientation, or in an attempted flight from it. The major contradiction in lack of education or negative information about homosexuality is that it produces a far greater toll of broken marriages and human misery: the very reason advanced for anti-homosexual stances, the 'protection of marriage and the family', in fact directly contributes to more marriage breakdowns where homosexuals have married. Ross confirms this in his third reason for marriage: social pressures, particularly from relatives, and from work. He makes the point that for job advancement, a 'normal' background, including marriage, may be required. It may also be required in order to keep relatives from becoming too suspicious.

The fourth reason advanced relates to a rational choice, particularly with regard to wanting to have children (there is no reason why homosexuals should not want children as much as any other individuals), companionship, and escape from loneliness. In these last two reasons one can again detect the hand of anti-homosexual propagandists, who maintain that to be homosexual is to be lonely, unwanted and unloved. It is a moot point whether such beliefs may not function as self-fulfilling prophesies: nevertheless, they still may push homosexuals into marriage. Finally, although this point is not covered by Ross, marriage may well be contracted by individuals who are genuine bisexuals (Kinsey Scale levels 2 and 3). Our concern, however, is for the predominantly homosexual male (Kinsey Scale levels 4, 5 and 6) rather than the genuine bisexual.

Some elaboration on these reasons was provided by H. L. Ross (1972): in this, he concentrates on the critical underlying issues. Labelling oneself as homosexual, he argues, depends on how, and whether, homosexual feelings are invested with significance. For example, he notes that all ten of the homosexuals he interviewed in Belgium were aware of attraction to members of their own sex prior to marriage, but did not consider themselves homosexual in the main. All their friends married, and they tended to do likewise. While all tried to fight their homosexual feelings during marriage, usually having a homosexual affair was what lead them to the identification of themselves as homosexual. In one case, the individual was jealous of his friend's romances and went to see a medical practitioner about it. The doctor indicated that it was just a 'stage he was going through', that he should find a nice girl and marry, and all would be well. Of course, it was not: this is one example of how some psychoanalytic perspectives of homosexuality as an arrested stage of development can lead to totally inappropriate clinical advice and management. Others chose marriage, Ross reports, deliberately, even though they knew sexual frustration would result. They were scared of loneliness, and of the current view that the Gay life was 'lonely and unpleasant'. Clearly, the public image of homosexuality was at fault, and when it was discovered that it was at fault, a re-evaluation of the marriage and sexual orientation took place.

Dank (1972) also looked at married homosexuals, and found that one quarter of his sample of sixty homosexual men in California had been married. He also concentrated on the underlying dynamics of the decision to marry, and particularly from the point of view of societal reaction theory, considering that 'traditional societal reaction against homosexuality is intimately related to the decision to marry.' As others have commented, and Dank elaborates, when an individual is raised in an anti-homosexual society, their socialisation is to a heterosexual, not a homosexual, role: the heterosexual role also includes marriage. The person with a homosexual orientation has a number of obstacles put in his way in terms of defining himself: he has no vocabulary with which to explain himself, and is forced to use a heterosexual one. He has access only to biased information on homosexuality, which indicates that such people are ill, criminal or perverted, things which he is not. He has access only to the common myth that homosexuals are effeminate, limp-wristed individuals who cross-dress in women's clothes from time to time and become hairdressers or interior decorators, which is also untrue in regard to himself. He may even learn that they are sexually attracted to young boys, which he is not. In sum, the result of inaccurate and negative information is to produce a model of the male homosexual which is so removed from reality as to make it impossible for homosexuals to identify themselves. Obviously the situation has improved markedly in the last decade: it remains to be seen whether the proportion of homosexual men marrying will show a similar decline.

In the context of such information, Dank notes, the homosexual may define himself as heterosexual or bisexual in order to preserve his positive self-concept and self-esteem: he cannot both be the monster of the myths and have a positive self-image. It is only when the meaning of the term 'homosexual' changes in a positive direction that the individual will define himself as one. Such a change in the meaning of the cognitive category, Dank notes, does not usually come until the individual meets other homosexuals and learns of, or is introduced into, the homosexual scene, and realises that homosexuals are ordinary people just like himself. This interpretation, which owes more to cognitive dissonance theory than to societal reaction theory, does appear to nicely account for the 'coming out' process in all homosexuals, not just married ones. At its core is the proposition that we cannot hold widely contradictory views about ourselves: one is either the homosexual of the myths and therefore a sick and depraved person, or the ordinary and capable individual one knows oneself to be. Since we know that we are worthwhile, we cannot therefore be homosexual; thus cognitive congruity is maintained.

Other myths also contribute to this sort of cognitive dissonance model. Silverstein and White (1977), for example, make the point that homosexuality is sometimes seen as just having sex with a man. If one can have sex with a woman, then one ceases to be homosexual. However, as Saghir and Robins (1973) note, some 48 per cent of their homosexual sample had had intercourse with a woman at some stage: average frequency of intercourse, while they were practising it, did not differ significantly between the homosexual and heterosexual groups. Also in the context of reasons for marriage, Saghir and Robins found that there was no significant difference between the homosexuals and the heterosexual control group in terms of being pursued by a woman: this had happened to about the same number of heterosexuals (39 per cent) and homosexuals (33 per cent) prior to the age of 20. Surprisingly, there was also no significant difference between the heterosexuals and homosexuals who had had intercourse in the duration of stable heterosexual relationships, with 78 per cent of both heterosexuals and homosexuals reporting that such a situation had occurred for one to three years, and in 22 per cent of both groups it had occurred for more than four years.

Clearly, from these data, homosexuals were, as much as heterosexuals, in a situation in which marriage might occur. One additional reason for marriage which is listed by Wafel-bakker (1975) along with the others already previously described is that of urging by the heterosexual partner. He notes that if she is aware of the homosexual tendencies of the partner, she often feels that marriage will cause them to disappear or at least diminish. If she is unaware of them, the sexual reticence of the male may well be an extra attraction for a woman who is sexually inhibited or puritanical, and therefore happy to do without premarital sexual contact. Given both this situation and the data provided by Saghir and Robins, it may be argued that it is not at all surprising that one in five homosexuals may marry, since they are almost as likely as heterosexuals to be living in a heterosexual relationship. The questions thus arise: how much is marriage in homosexuals a function of social or societal pressure? How much is it a result of a natural progression in a relationship? How much is it a result of the man not knowing he is homosexual?

A second set of questions relates to what happens within the marriage, in terms of adjustment and consequences. At a general level, Imieliński (1969), reporting on twenty-eight married male homosexuals in Poland from 1946 to 1961, indicates that the higher their position on the Kinsey Scale (that is, the more homosexual they were), the shorter the marriage. The marriages he reports in homosexuals ranged in length from several weeks to continuing relationships: there were, however, no continuing marriages with homosexuality of level 4 or above, and only limited continuing marriages at levels 1 and 2, predominantly heterosexual. When one recalls that some 37 per cent of males fall into level 1 (incidental homosexual experience), these figures are a little surprising. Like other authors, Imieliński notes that two of his sample married on the advice of their medical practitioner to 'cure them of their perversions'! Reasons for marriage in his twenty-eight men included advice of a medical practitioner that marriage would remove their 'perversion' (9), desire for children and to remove their homosexuality (8), emotional relationships with women (5), desire for home help (4), and no reason (2). The majority of these individuals, therefore, were attempting to get rid of their homosexual preference. From his evidence, however, it seems clear that the more homosexual one is, the less chance of marriage succeeding and, probably, the shorter its duration.

H. L. Ross (1971, 1972) has documented the sources of conflict and modes of adjustment in marriage. Most of the problems, he indicates, were sexual. As the marriage progressed, sexual relations between husband and wife decreased markedly, often to the stage where they occurred once a month, or never. Husbands apparently argued that their wives had little need for sex, but the wives strongly disputed this: they felt defrauded and resentful, particularly when they found out about their husband's sexual orientation after marriage. Where homosexual relationships did occur, if they were other than ephemeral, they were bitterly resented, especially if a long-term intimate relationship did develop. The husbands asserted that they would accept it if their wives had outside affairs, but this statement appeared to be made in the knowledge that this would never be put to the test! Conflicts tended to develop in the area of sexuality and to spill over into other domestic areas. Lateness or unexplained absences lead to suspicions and recriminations on the part of the wife, and general marital disharmony.

The adjustments made to this, as previously indicated, included separation, platonic marriage, the double-standard marriage, and the innovative marriage. Separation tended not to occur if there were children, and particularly, if there were such non-sexual satisfactions such as a home, division of labour, companionship, or a fear of living alone, and need for social respect. Platonic marriage usually included the husband having casual sex on the side, which the wife was unaware of: she may also be unaware of her husband's sexual orientation. Both partners tended to concentrate on such non-sexual interests as children and job. The double-standard marriage included an overt liaison between the husband and his lover outside the marriage, and his visiting both his lover's place

31

and his own home back and forth. Needless to say, this was greatly resented by the wife, who accepted it only because it was the only way to keep the marriage intact. Finally, Ross reports one case of the innovative marriage, in which both partners engaged in outside affairs, but in which marital sex always played a big part. There was also the occasional ménage à trois: however, it would appear that this particular marriage was successful because the sexual and affective bonds between the partners were still strong. Perhaps the most important thing to note in the examples given by Ross is that all these adjustments occurred in a climate of near-complete acceptance of conventional norms. Clearly, the situation in Catholic Belgium in 1970 will be different from the situation in less traditional communities. Wafelbakker (1975), for example, writes not of permanent adjustments so much as of stages which merge into one another. From the course of the first years of marriage, in which sexual contact becomes more infrequent and incidental homosexual contacts may occur, the relationship may develop towards an unmasking of the husband's sexual orientation. During a frank talk with the spouse, which itself may be stimulated by exposure which is out of the husband's control, seeing a particular film or documentary, a need to break the news of a homosexual affair, or simply a need for frank communication, there may be a tremendous sense of relief and removal of emotional stress. All kinds of behaviour by the homosexual partner suddenly became clear, according to Wafelbakker: the going to bed late, the irritability, the over-active social life.

At first, he suggests, the frank talk offers a form of security, along with a feeling of solidarity and the ability to solve the problem together. On the other hand, there may also be disbelief and disgust on the part of the spouse, who may take weeks or months to accept the idea, or refuse to discuss it further. Whatever happens, the problems have now shifted from the homosexual to the heterosexual partner, who may feel they cannot trust the husband, and doubt whether he has ever loved them. Others may feel used and resentful. Divorce is considered in many cases; in only a few cases does it actually occur. Wafelbakker notes that the same mechanisms which lead to marriage may also be partly active in preserving marriage, for example, the need for security, companionship and social respectability. Nevertheless, emergency and short-term solutions such as separation for a month or several weeks, a certain degree of freedom for homosexual contacts, are often discussed. Such solutions are usually short-term because of jealousy and resentment by the spouse at the homosexual contacts, and because of loneliness from separation. If there is an on-going homosexual relationship outside the marriage, however, separation is often likely to become permanent. Both partners will have strong guilt feelings, particularly the husband, at the thought that the marriage may be dissolved because of his own role in discussing the matter and his sexual orientation. Similarly, the spouse may be overtly antagonistic and accusatory.

In a more detailed series of five case studies which looked at coping with homosexual expression within heterosexual marriage, Latham and White (1978) looked at the stages of adjustment within the marriages (of the five cases, all the husbands and one wife were homosexual, and with one exception still living together). They present an heuristic model to describe the stages of adjustment in a marriage with one homosexual partner. However, it is important to note that in their sample of five cases, all the spouses were aware of their husband's homosexuality, and all the men had reportedly married for 'internally motivated' reasons: to have a family life and children. As Latham and White point out, there is no reason why such reasons as having children and close heterosexual relationships should be sacrificed simply because of the presence of homosexuality, and we should not let an individual's sexual preference colour all other aspects of his functioning. On the other hand, the contradiction between homosexual preference and heterosexual marriage is a direct one, and cannot be lightly ignored. Significantly, all the men in Latham and White's sample rated themselves on average at level 3.2 on the Kinsey Scale at the time of their marriage: that is, attracted equally to males and females. At the time of the study, however, they rated themselves on average at level 4.4, a significant increase. The average length of marriage in this study was 12.6 years, with a range of 2 to 27.5. Other characteristics of these five cases were interesting: in all cases the spouse knew of the husband's homosexuality at the time of marriage, in all cases there was premarital sex, and in almost all cases (one exception) the couples had children, and were still living together. All the wives had had extramarital affairs, and all were still having sex within the marriage. In this respect, they were all rather like the 'innovative marriage' described by Ross (1971).

The three phases described by Latham and White were withdrawal-avoidance, disclosure-acceptance, and adjustment-coping. Withdrawal-avoidance, ranging from one to five years, was the period when the husband avoided homosexual contacts, or had clandestine and guilt-ridden contacts. Often during this phase the husband's homosexuality became a scapegoat for problems experienced elsewhere in the marriage. The disclosure-acceptance stage marked the point where the partners in the marriage began to establish coping patterns in order to continue the marriage. What anxiety and guilt that did occur in this stage was reported to be predominantly because of the contradiction of the societally accepted standard of monogamy. Renegotiation of the marriage at this point was either an on-going process or a response to crisis, such as the arrest of the husband on a sex-related charge. Transition was least traumatic the greater the degree of on-going heterosexual contact in the marriage, which suggests again that degree of homosexuality, and heterosexuality, is the crucial mediating event in continuation of a successful marriage. Adjustment-coping as the final stage was characterised by a greater degree of sexual expression by both husband and wife outside the marriage: several couples indicated that the issue was more one of open marriage than sexual preference. Conflict within the marriage was much less often linked to sexual preference, compared with the first stage in which divorce was often discussed. At this third stage, what appeared to have happened was that the couple had established guidelines for behaviour to govern the rules for outside sexual contacts. Those couples who cannot establish mutually acceptable rules presumably separate. Such rules include those relating to having outside contacts within the home, meeting them socially, and degree of disclosure of such contacts to the spouse.

Latham and White conclude that the success of marriage is likely to be greatest in those marrying for internally motivated reasons, and in those couples who can work at a set of mutually acceptable guidelines regarding an open marriage. What is most evident in their five case histories is that despite most of the men being at least bisexual on marriage, the homosexual component of their sexual preference did not wane, but in fact increased in strength in all of them. The suggestion is made, however, that were adoption available to single individuals or same-sex couples more readily, the number of people marrying for these 'internally motivated' reasons may well decrease. All but one of the couples Latham and White interviewed had children.

Results of marriages of homosexuals have, however, not usually been as positive as the five couples Latham and White describe. Ross (1971, 1972) documents the continuation of the marriages as being, in the case of platonic marriages, the source of mutual dissatisfaction and displacement of interest from the marital bond, with consequent sexual and psychological frustration. Mutual dissatisfaction, and as a consequence mutual guilt, was frequently expressed. The double-standard marriage shifted the price of conflict on to the heterosexual partner, along with the bitterness and jealousy that she naturally felt. Only the innovative marriage, which depended on the versatility of the wife, appeared to work. As Ross sums up his research, the social advantages in marrying are bought at a high price in unhappiness. Acceptance of social norms by homosexual men marrying is apparently compounded by couples continuing to live together after the marriage has clearly become unviable for the same reason: fear of transgressing social norms.

Reasons for ending the marriage, according to Saghir and Robins (1973), include emotional and sexual dissatisfaction: ultimately, the conflict between homosexual psychological and sexual needs and the heterosexual demands of marriage caught up with the couple, although having a child did tend to keep marriages together somewhat longer. However, Imieliński reports that although eleven of his sample of twenty-eight married, seven of these ultimately divorced.

So far, only studies which interview married homosexuals who admit to being homosexual have been reviewed. There are one or two studies, however, which looked at the married homosexual outside the context of his sexuality. While the research of Humphreys (1970) has already been referred to previously, some interesting findings are reported in passing by Neill, Marshall and Yale (1978). These authors were looking at the partners of individuals who were grossly obese and as a consequence had intestinal bypass surgery to rectify this. As a result of the surgery, the twelve women they report on lost considerable weight and became much more attractive. This in turn resulted in a degree of marital disharmony when the husbands of these women became threatened by the fact that their spouses were now attractive (including to other men), and thus feared being abandoned for more attractive men. Sex also began to play a much greater part in the marital relationship following bypass surgery and weight loss. Of particular interest, however, is the fact that three out of the twelve husbands (one quarter) became homosexual after their wives' weight loss.

The dynamics of the situation is probably this: men with homosexual tendencies who wished to de-emphasise or remove them may have chosen as a partner a woman who was massively obese. Such a partner would probably have a lower need for sex, and being seen as unattractive and thus undesirable, be less inclined to question low frequency of sexual contact within marriage. On becoming attractive and expressing her sexual needs more openly, the latently homosexual husband was probably forced to confront his inability to cope with marital sexual interaction and thus his homosexuality. What this study does suggest is that there may be a number of instances which other studies do not touch on, of marriages of homosexual men which are never subject to examination, and thus allow a biased picture to be presented in terms of those which are reported.

The picture which is presented so far does imply that marriages which involve homosexual men are, in the main, likely to be unsuccessful, and that a homosexual orientation dooms marriage. On the other hand, there is also some suggestion that adjustments may be made if both partners are able to live within an open marriage, and if the husband is predominantly bisexual and able to function heterosexually within marriage. However, the studies of Humphreys suggest that there are numerous married homosexual men in the community who are living within stable and reasonably adequate marriages, and Neill, Marshall and Yale also imply that there are a number of marriages in which the marital dynamics mask the fact that the husband is homosexual until some major marital readjustment forces their sexual preference to the surface. Sampling problems, which preclude one tapping such sources, also preclude easy answers to the question of adjustment within such marriages, given that the only samples available are usually those individuals who have acknowledged their sexual orientation to others and who are known in the Gay scene.

Reasons for marriage, nevertheless, do show a considerable preponderance of 'externally' motivated, relating to social pressures of one sort or another, or secondary manifestations of social pressures. Of course, it could also be argued that since the 'internally' motivated marriages have a greater chance of success, according to Latham and White, there is a preponderance of external pressures to marriage reflected in those men who are sampled via the Gay scene. Clearly, there is a great need for many of the questions, explicit and implicit, raised in the rather sketchy research on small numbers to date, to be raised in a controlled fashion with a larger group of married homosexual men.

4 The present study: method and scope

Study one

The present study set out to try to answer five basic questions about the married homosexual man. First, is he different from other homosexual males in his relating to the homosexual subculture and heterosexual world and in his psychological adjustment? Second, is the marriage situation a result of immediate background factors and situations in terms of demographic variables; personality-based (that is, a type of homosexual who is likely to marry can be identified); or not connected with any identifiable events or personality types? Third, given that there must be some role or sexual conflict with a predominantly homosexual male in a heterosexual marriage situation, what sort of adjustments and adaptations occur, and how common are they? Fourth, what is the role of societal reaction in the adjustment and social interaction of the homosexual male? And, finally, if any of the above questions show that the married homosexual male has reacted to social pressure in any way differently from the non-married sample, can this be generalised, either theoretically or practically, to other homosexuals who have problems adapting to social pressures either expected or apparent?

Within these five areas, a number of specific questions can be formulated. These are grouped according to their implications into three areas: first, those which hypothesise causes of marriage in homosexuals; second, those dealing with its effects; and third, hypotheses which do not directly fall into any of the two above categories and which address incidental questions generated from the literature on the phenomenon which has been surveyed.

There are six questions which relate to causal aspects:

(1) That homosexual men who have married are psychologically less resistant to social pressure and less psychologically well adjusted.
(2) That those respondents who recognised their homosexuality before marriage, married in an attempt to play down their homosexuality.
(3) That those respondents who married will show a high acceptance of conventional norms compared with those who never married.
(4) That of those respondents who married, the majority will have married at under 25, and that loneliness will be reported as a major factor in marriage of these respondents.
(5) That a high proportion of the respondents who married will have attempted to change their orientation compared with those respondents who never married.
(6) That the main reasons given for marriage will be reasons of social, family or partner pressure.

Three questions relate to effects of marriage in homosexuals.

(1) That those respondents who reported recognising their homosexuality only after marriage will show differences in degree of expected negative societal reaction and psychological adjustment from those who recognised their orientation before marriage.
(2) That those respondents who married will be the most secretive about their orientation.
(3) That any lack of psychological adjustment in respondents will be a result of marriage and other such immediate stresses rather than caused by any recognisable personality type.

The remaining six research questions are incidental to cause and effect testing hypotheses raised in overseas research:

(1) That scores on conservatism measures will differentiate between those respondents who are high and low in

their resistance to social pressure.

(2) That those respondents who report themselves bisexual will show better adjustment on the individual items and scales of psychological adjustment than those reporting themselves as predominantly homosexual.

(3) That those respondents who do not appear obviously homosexual will show better adjustment on the psychological scales.

(4) That those respondents with high commitment to homosexuality will conceive homosexuality as more normal than those with low commitment.

(5) That of the married sample, a high proportion of the wives will be aware of their husband's orientation because of the overt-sample bias.

(6) That those respondents who have married will show no significant decrease in the degree of their homosexuality.

'Psychological adjustment' was defined in terms of the nine sub-scales of psychological adjustment used by Weinberg and Williams (1974) (Appendix 2). These sub-scales, although described in detail in the appendices for those who have a particular interest in the research methodology and psychometrics, are as follows: self-acceptance, stability of self-concept, depression, anxiety, interpersonal awkwardness, faith in others, loneliness and psychiatric experience and psychosomatic symptoms. Other measures contained in the questionnaire used by Weinberg and Williams (1974) and included in the present research include being known about in the heterosexual world, anticipated discrimination, expected attitudes toward homosexuals, passing as heterosexual, being labelled as homosexual, social involvement with heterosexuals, social identification as heterosexual or homosexual, traditional values and perceived breach of them by homosexuality, social involvement with homosexuals, acculturation to the Gay scene, sexual practices, frequency of homosexual contact, the Kinsey Scale, homosexual social situation, homosexual relationships, homosexual commitment, conception of homosexuality as normal and conception of homosexuality in terms of responsibility.

Method

The sample of sixty-three was divided into three groups of twenty-one respondents each. Group 1: homosexual males still married and living with their wives; Group 2: homosexual males who were separated, divorced or widowed; and Group 3: homosexual males who had never been married.

In order to control for any variables which might influence results, respondents were matched on age, educational level, socio-economic status and occupation. Since Group 3 (the 'control' group) were to be compared with Groups 1 and 2 combined, not as separate groups, and since obtaining control respondents who matched those in Groups 1 and 2 on all matching variables, especially age, was difficult, a split matching technique was adopted. All Group 1 and 2 respondents were split into small groups for each variable to be matched. Educational level was divided into five sub-groups corresponding to the divisions on the questionnaire used (high school, university entrance examination, some university, degree, graduate degree); age into eight sub-groups of five years from 20 to the last sub-group of 56+; socio-economic status into the four sub-groups in the questionnaire (upper, upper middle, lower middle and working class); and occupation into four sub-groups of professional, managerial/sales, clerical, skilled labour and working. Each of these sub-groups was in turn split in half in terms of their number and respondents selected who conformed on each matching variable to the now halved number of 21. Thus the proportion of 'control' respondents in any group or sub-group remained identical with that in the same combined group of the married and previously married sample. In this way, respondents were matched altering nothing but the number of the 'control' sample.

Married and previously married respondents were obtained in three ways: first, by contacting those people with whom the researcher was personally acquainted and requesting them to complete the questionnaire anonymously and post it back; second, by requesting all those personal acquaintances and contacts in the homosexual subculture throughout New Zealand and Melbourne, Australia, to pass questionnaires on to any people who might be willing to participate in the study to be completed and returned anonymously; and third, by inserting an advertisement in the New Zealand *Gay News* and the newsletter of the New Zealand Homosexual Law Reform Society which read:

MARRIED AND PREVIOUSLY MARRIED
HOMOSEXUALS:
Research is currently being carried out on homosexual men who have at any time been heterosexually married, or are still married. As many people as possible are asked to assist, either by agreeing to be interviewed or by replying to a questionnaire. If you know of any such people, it would be appreciated if their attention could be drawn to this. Any information collected will of course remain strictly confidential and be used for research purposes only; individuals will in no way be identifiable in any publication which may result. With these assurances your cooperation is looked forward to. Please contact: (the researcher's name and University address followed).

Of fifty-nine questionnaires distributed to Groups 1 and 2, forty-two (71 per cent) were returned, as against the 78 per cent return rate for the 'control' group. Data was collected in 1975.

The questionnaire was adapted from that used by Weinberg and Williams (1974) with minor additions obtaining more data specifically on the married or previously married respondent. The questionnaire was thus predominantly in a form tested previously with a sample of 2,347. Four main scales were included in the questionnaire form: psychological adjustment (eight sub-scales); relating to the heterosexual world (nine sub-scales); relating to the homosexual world (ten sub-scales); and the biographical data section. The Wilson-Patterson conservatism scale (Wilson, 1973) was also included. A breakdown of the questionnaire by item and scale is included in Appendix 2.

Data was computer analysed by the Statistical Package for the Social Sciences (SPSS). For each scale where such a computation was appropriate, mean and standard deviation were computed for Groups 1 and 2 combined and Group 3. Cross-tabulation with chi-square was also carried out on individual items where appropriate. The results of these data analyses are presented in the appropriate appendix in table form. After analysis of this first study on married homosexual men in New Zealand and in south-east Australia, a second study was carried out on homosexual men generally in Australia (east coast), Sweden and Finland. This second study contained questions which asked if respondents had been married, were presently married, or had been engaged to be married. In this way, it was possible to get an indication of the extent of the phenomenon in different countries, and to check on some of the data obtained in the first study.

Study two

The second study was part of a larger study on homosexuality in three cultures: Sweden, Finland and Australia. While the questionnaire contained many of the same questions as in Study One, there were no specific questions relating to reasons for, or adaptation to, marriage, and no attempt was made to select married homosexual men. Thus an estimate of the proportion of married homosexual men across three societies could be made using the same questionnaire. In addition, many of the general hypotheses put forward in the literature and in the first study could be tested in different cultural settings and on a larger sample.

Sweden, Finland and Australia were chosen for several reasons. Chief among these was the fact that all three are industrialised and affluent Western societies, of a roughly similar size (Sweden 9 million, Australia 13 million, Finland 4 million population). The Australian sample was selected from two east coast states, Queensland (population 2½ million) and Victoria (population 3½ million).

The other reason for selection related to attitudes toward homosexuality and attitudes toward sex roles and the status of the female. Sweden is both accepting of homosexuality (the laws proscribing it were removed in 1944) and has strong legislated support for equality between males and females. Finland has a similar attitude toward equality between the sexes, while being anti-homosexual in that

43

although homosexual acts between consenting adults are legal, it is illegal to talk about homosexuality in any other than a negative way. In both Victoria and Queensland at the time of data collection in Australia, homosexual acts were criminal and there was little legislation which dealt with equality between the sexes: in fact, one writer (McKenzie, 1962) has commented that women in Australia have a less significant role in the professions and in public life and encounter more formal and informal discrimination than in any other industrial democracy. Given these differences, it is possible to test, to a limited degree, the hypothesis that the social environment of homosexuals is likely to affect the proportion of homosexuals who marry.

The second purpose of the second study was to test the validity and reliability of the major findings in other Western cultures and in other samples. If these findings can be reproduced in such a fashion, it will confirm that some general comments may in fact be made about the married homosexual man in Western society. However, it is not intended to go into great detail in the second study, but to concentrate on epidemiology, psychological adjustment and the influence of societal reaction in married homosexuals.

Method

The samples were all collected in 1978, and consisted of 176 Swedish, 163 Australian and 149 Finnish homosexual men. All three samples were obtained by enclosing the research questionnaire, which had been translated into the appropriate language (Swedish and Finnish) and then translated back by a second individual as a check to ensure accuracy, with the newsletters of the main homosexual social-rights organisation in the respective cities. These cities were Stockholm (population 1 million), Helsinki (population ½ million), Melbourne (population 3 million) and Brisbane (population 1 million). In each case, the organisation was the only, or the major, homosexual organisation in the city and also functioned as the main national or state organisation. Return rates were 44 per cent for Sweden, 46.6 per cent for Australia and 54 per cent for Finland, and is based on the number of questionnaires given to the clubs to mail, equivalent to the number of males on their mailing list. In all cases, the aims of the societies appeared equivalent to each other.

The sample subjects, on the basis of questions asking 'Have you ever been married?', 'Have you ever been engaged?', 'Are you still married?', 'Are you separated, divorced or a widower?', were divided into five groups. Group 1 was those who had ever been married; Group 2 was those who were still married; Group 3 was those who had previously, but were not at present, married; Group 4 was those who had been engaged but not married, and Group 5 was those who had never been involved with a woman (ever married or engaged). The remainder constituted the control group. The main analyses completed were between those still married and those separated (Groups 2 and 3); between those who had ever been married and the unmarried controls (Group 1 and controls); and between those who had ever been involved with a woman (Groups 1 and 4 combined and controls).

The questionnaire items which were analysed included those which were identical to those used in Study One, although the total questionnaire contained a number of other items which were different and part of a larger study (Ross, 1980, 1983a). Reference in the text will therefore be to item numbers in the Study One questionnaire. Data analysis was again by the SPSS computer package, and again utilised t-tests for data which was measured on an interval or ratio scale, and chi-square for data on nominal or ordinal scales. In addition, one-way analyses of variance (fixed effects model) were used where it was necessary to make comparisons between the three cultures.

The results (see Table 4.1) indicate that there were no significant differences between the three samples on age, years of education, age at which respondents became homosexually active, age at which respondents realised they were homosexual, or position on the Kinsey Scale. There were, however, significant differences between the three samples in two variables, religion and social class of parents. The differences in degree of religious interest can be explained

Table 4.1 **Sample characteristics, Study Two**

	Australia	*Sweden*	*Finland*	*Significance*
Age	32.0 ± 11.4	30.9 ± 7.4	28.4 ± 7.8	n.s.
Years education	13.3 ± 3.6	12.7 ± 5.3	13.2 ± 4.4	n.s.
Age at which became homosexually active	19.3 ± 12.1	20.8 ± 7.4	20.4 ± 7.2	n.s.
Age realised was homosexual	12.5 ± 7.0	14.1 ± 5.7	13.9 ± 5.4	n.s.
Kinsey Scale level	6.7 ± 1.0	6.6 ± 0.8	6.5 ± 0.9	n.s.
Religion: practising	52	11	10	
nominal	51	91	66	
none	49	62	64	$p < .01$
Social class of parents:				
upper	8	32	4	
middle	89	80	66	
lower	56	57	74	$p < .01$

n.s. = not significant at $p < .10$

by the fact that some of the Australian sample were contacted through the Metropolitan Community Church, a Christian church with a predominantly homosexual membership. There is no equivalent in Sweden and Finland. The higher proportion of Swedes who reported upper-class parents, out of proportion to the Australian and Finnish sample, is difficult to explain, although it may be that Sweden has a much stronger aristocratic tradition than the other two countries. However, were these class differences genuine and significant, it would be expected that there would also be educational differences between the samples, which was not the case. It is difficult to see how the social class differences between the samples could systematically affect the results.

The sample in Study Two was gathered as part of a larger research project in order to check the representativeness of the findings of Study One across cultures and with different samples and in order to get an overview of the place and prevalence of married homosexuals in the wider homosexual subculture: results are reported of this second study in Chapter 11.

5 Comparison of still married and separated homosexuals

In order to determine whether it is the marriage situation (that is, being still married and living with one's wife) which causes the difficulties in adjustment which have been hypothesised in married homosexuals, or whether it is general to those who have at any time been married, it is necessary to compare the still married sample with the formerly married sample. In this way, the effects of being still married can be assessed, while holding constant the fact that both samples have at some stage been married and therefore holding constant the type of person who is likely to get married. Consequently, personality and predisposition to marry are controlled for, and what is seen from the comparison of the still married and formerly married samples is the effect of being in the marriage situation on the homosexual man.

While the differences between the separated and still married homosexuals and the total married group and the non-married controls do not conform exactly to the pattern stated in the hypotheses, it is readily apparent that a number of significant differences between groups, which fit into the general form of the hypotheses, have been found. It will be remembered that it was hypothesised that the homosexual men still married would be less well adjusted psychologically and less involved in the homosexual world. Discussion is divided into four sub-sections for clarity and ease of analysis: psychological adjustment; situation amongst homosexuals; situation amongst heterosexuals; and background of respondent. However, where necessary, other aspects from separate sections are discussed to illustrate trends and further hypotheses as these arise.

With regard to the respondents who have been married at some time, further divided into two categories, those not now living with their wives and those still living with their wives (twenty-one in each group), there are a number of interesting differences and similarities in biographical and background data. While the married groups were matched on age with the never married sample, within the two married samples there was no matching. However, there was little difference between mean age for the still and formerly married samples, 41.4 and 37.8 respectively. This rules out the possibility that the still married group remained married because of either greater age-linked conservatism, or greater pressure against expression of homosexuality in the more distant past. The other matching variables of educational level, occupation and socio-economic level also show no bias with regard to either group. Of the formerly married respondents, 50 per cent were living alone, while 20 per cent lived in a flat with other homosexuals and a further 20 per cent permanently with a homosexual partner. None were living with women: this could suggest a definite homosexual commitment, more so as none of the unmarried group were living permanently with a homosexual partner in the same residence. This is discussed at greater length below.

Place of residence is significantly different between the formerly and still married groups: while 75 per cent of the formerly married group had lived in a large or medium city in their teenage years, 68 per cent of those still married had spent their adolescence in a town or the country. One could suggest that, while there may be greater pressure to marry in the more conservative rural areas, there is also more pressure to stay married in such areas, or, alternatively, to move to metropolitan areas after separation. This latter point is borne out by looking at place of present residence: 75 per cent of those separated live in a large city compared with 36 per cent of those still married. None of the formerly married sample currently lives in a town, while 27 per cent of the still married sample do, the differences being statistically significant.

The further background variable of religion shows one interesting result. While there are no significant differences between groups on religious affiliation or degree of religious commitment at the present time, the degree of religious commitment of the parent shows a difference between the two groups at $p < .03$, with the parents of those remaining married tending to have a higher commitment to religion. While one cannot suggest that this might have had any influence on the decision to marry, as it is not reflected in a difference between the combined sample of the formerly and still married homosexual men and the control sample of those never married, it might be argued that a higher degree of religious commitment on the part of the parents may lead to a greater reluctance to break up a marriage, possibly as a result of strongly impressed 'sanctity of marriage' beliefs of the parents. This tends to be confirmed further on in the questionnaire, where still married respondents rate formal religion as more important to them than do those who have separated.

While degree of homosexuality is discussed in a later chapter, it is worthy of note here that, on the two Kinsey Scales (behavioural and self-rating), degree of homosexuality and marriage situation are statistically significant for both scales: significantly more formerly married respondents were in the last two categories of the scale (totally or predominantly homosexual in orientation). Thus it would appear that, the higher the degree of homosexuality, the more likely the marriage is to break up. There was also some tendency for the age of marriage in the formerly married group to be lower than in the still married group (mean ages 24.6 and 28.8 respectively). Possibly this difference may reflect a greater maturity, or having thought the problem out better, in the case of still married respondents, leading to a tendency to stay together longer. Since there are no significant differences between groups with regard to the proportion who knew of their homosexuality before and after marriage, it cannot be argued that the younger mean age in the formerly married men represents a greater proportion of respondents who were unaware of their homosexual tendencies. Similarly, in regard to whether there is any difference between groups on whether the spouse was told of her husband's homosexuality before the marriage, after, or never, there is no difference.

49

The difference in age of marriage would, therefore, seem to be best interpreted as a function of increased maturity and consideration of the situation at the time of marriage.

The mean length of marriage for the formerly married group was 6.1 years, still married 17.3 years (and still continuing). That the marriages of the separated sample respondents lasted as long as six years on average indicates that some time was spent making the attempt to continue with a satisfactory marriage — however, the lower median of 3.5 years emphasises that most marriages were comparatively short-lived. Mean time of separation was 6.7 years.

It is interesting to note that, in terms of degree of homosexuality, 70 per cent of the married respondents (both groups) indicated that they felt their degree of homosexuality had remained the same; 25 per cent considered they had become more homosexual as a result of marriage, 5 per cent less. While much has been made of the value of optimum social situation for a homosexual to change his orientation with positive reinforcers and full opportunities for heterosexual sex and partnership, even in such an optimum situation as marriage, only 5 per cent report any lessening of their homosexual urges. The number reporting an increase of homosexuality (25 per cent) is, given the circumstances, not very surprising, as marriage presumably forced the choice on these respondents, and their homosexuality predominated. One possible factor which could account for some of the permanency of the still continuing marriages is the number of children born to the marriage: all of these respondents had children (mean 2.8 each), whereas only 57 per cent of the separated respondents had offspring (mean 1.8 each). The higher number of children in the still married group is probably a function of the greater time spent in marriage, though.

Reasons given for marriage show no particular trends for either group. However, they are a good indication of the sort of pressures and motivations acting on homosexual men (see Table 5.1). In rank order, the first most common main reason for marriage was 'I was "in love"' (26.2 per cent). The high ranking could be accounted for to some extent by the number of the total of both married samples (33 per cent)

Table 5.1 **Reasons given for marriage**

Statement	% as main reason
You were 'in love'	26.2
You thought your homosexuality would go if you married	16.7
Wife pregnant	11.9
Pressure from girlfriend	11.9
You wanted children and family life	7.1
It seemed the natural thing	7.1
Everyone else was getting married	4.8
All other reasons	12.0

who said they were not aware of their homosexuality until after their marriage. Nevertheless, the idea of marrying because one is 'in love' tends to suggest the romantic notion of falling in love, getting married and living happily ever after, which has become such a stereotype and goal that it almost reaches the level of a 'social pressure'. If one has not been 'in love' before the end of one's teens, one may be considered rather strange. But in a number of cases, obviously, it was the genuine reason for the marriage, which, in many cases, has continued and in which an element of 'love' still plays some part.

The second most common main reason given (16.7 per cent) was that the respondent 'thought his homosexuality might go'. This high ranking is similar to Dannecker and Reiche's results (1974), in which 56 per cent marked responses which implied an attempt to hide or throw off their homosexuality. Third equal in ranking in the present study (11.9 per cent each) were two similar reasons: pressure from girlfriend and future wife's pregnancy. It is very possible that the latter leads to the former! However, both imply further pressure or coercion from an external source. Pressure from wife was ranked rather lower in Dannecker and Reiche's data (seventh): this may be a function of the less traditional society in New Zealand and Australia.

Ranked fourth equal (7.1 per cent each) were the statements 'You wanted children', and 'It seemed the natural thing.' The ranking of the last statement is similar to that in the West German data, in which this reason also fell into the top three ranks. Since children are probably one of the few things in a relationship that homosexual couples cannot have compared with heterosexual couples, it is no surprise that some may get married for this reason. Many of the arguments used for the first-ranked statement (You were 'in love') also apply to 'It seemed the natural thing': it is part of the social stereotype, and unless one conforms, whether by doing the 'natural thing' or by falling 'in love', one would tend to be identified as unusual.

A very similar reason occurs in fifth rank: 'Everyone else was getting married' (4.8 per cent). This could, to some extent, be equated with the reason given sixth rank in the West German data, social obligations. The surprising point is the low ranking (fifth equal) of the reason 'Companionship', which occurred first in the list of Dannecker and Reiche. The marriage reasons for the present married samples appear to concentrate heavily on aspects which could be generally described as either social (in terms of social expectancy) or an attempt to remove their homosexuality: there seems to be a noticeable trend for those respondents who were aware of their orientation to have married because of either specific or general concern over their homosexuality.

However, while 'companionship' holds a low rank on the scale of reasons for marriage, on the scale of 'Best things about marriage' (Table 5.2) it holds first rank. As this scale was an open one inviting responses, it is perhaps significant that, while all the still married respondents answered, only 87 per cent of the formerly married respondents could think of any good things about marriage. It seems even more significant that there was a tendency for the still married respondents to mark the first two factors (companionship and children) more often than the separated group who marked factors 3 and 4 (shared experiences and status) as the best things about marriage. It would appear that those who remained married were more able to take the non-affective factors of marriage and build on them, whereas the separated

Table 5.2 **Best things about marriage**

Separated Statement	%	Still married Statement	%
Companionship	37.5	Companionship	45.0
Shared experiences, someone to talk to	31.3	Children	40.0
		Being loved	5.0
		Having things done	5.0
Status	12.5	Shared experiences, someone to	
Children	12.5		
Being loved	6.3	talk to	5.0

group were not able to find anything better than sharing experiences and status in marriage. This could well be a function of the greater maturity, which it was earlier suggested could be a result of the still married respondents marrying considerably later than the formerly married respondents: with later marriage, there would seem to be fewer illusions about the situation and greater will to make the best of the things about marriage worth keeping the marriage together for.

As with the best things about a marriage, the worst things about marriage (Table 5.3), in a similar open-ended question form, was responded to by all of the separated group, but by only 89 per cent of the still married group. There was little variation between groups, though, on the factors noted. While 'loss of freedom' may be regarded as one of the worst things about marriage by many men who marry, whether homosexual or not, 'sex' as a response, while indicating the predominant homosexuality of the majority of the sample, also bears out the point that it is the respondents who make the most of the non-sexual aspects of marriage who tend to have the marriage continue, as 'sex' seems to be a disliked aspect of marriage with both groups of the married sample, although much more so by the separated group. It may well be that success of marriage is related to the ability to derive some heterosexual satisfaction from the marriage and this degree of homosexuality: this is in line with the findings of Imieliński (1969).

Table 5.3 **Worst things about marriage**

Separated Statement	%	*Still married* Statement	%
Sex	31.6	Loss of freedom	41.2
Loss of freedom	15.8	Having to stay home	29.4
Lack of finance	15.8	Double life	17.6
Double life	10.5	Sex	11.8
Having to stay home	10.5		
Having to go out with wife	10.5		
Wife's family	5.3		

On the question 'Did your homosexuality become more important to you at any stage of marriage?', 38 per cent replied no, 62 per cent yes, with no differences between groups. Thus, with no significant differences between groups, one cannot point to homosexuality as such as the factor which caused the marriages to break up. Rather, it would appear that the still married respondents could better cope with their homosexuality within marriage, a supposition which fits in well with the group of factors discussed earlier suggesting greater maturity in this group. Of those respondents who answered yes, reasons for this were ranked in Table 5.4. Interestingly, the responses throw some additional light on earlier suggestions of differences in maturity of respondents in the married sample. There was some tendency for formerly married respondents to give the factor 'marriage strains' as a response, whereas still married respondents tended more often to rank the most commonly responded to factor 'You couldn't keep your homosexual feelings at bay'. General marriage strains seem to be less common in the marriages of the still married sample and it was the reported homosexuality as such which tended to cause the upsurge in interest in homosexuality at some time during the marriage with this group. While 'Meeting a particular Gay person' was a common reason given, there is no significant difference between the two groups of the married samples on this: it could be emphasised that a particular interpersonal attraction between two people must take place in a

Table 5.4 **Reasons for increase in importance of homosexuality during marriage**

Separated Statement	%	Still Married Statement	%
Marriage strains	35.7	Couldn't keep homosexual feelings at bay	53.3
Couldn't keep homosexual feelings at bay	28.6	Meeting a particular Gay person	26.7
Meeting a particular Gay person	14.3	Wife's frigidity	13.3
Wife's frigidity	14.3	Marriage began to grow stale	7.1
Marriage began to grow stale	7.1		

homosexual as well as a heterosexual situation before a significant relationship can develop, and simply mixing in a homosexual subculture and having sex is not necessarily enough for a person's homosexuality to become more important to them.

Very surprisingly, 32 per cent of the separated group reported they had thought of remarriage: whether this is a result of further susceptibility to social pressures or a seeking for a companionship is not apparent at this stage.

Significant differences are also apparent between the groups on the question 'Do you currently have a regular homosexual partner?'. 63 per cent of the separated group replied yes, as did 22 per cent of those still married. While this discrepancy is not surprising in terms of opportunities available, the percentage for those still married indicates that, for almost a quarter of the currently married respondents, a regular homosexual partner was a way of adjusting to the situation of heterosexual marriage. Compared with the control (never married) sample the proportion answering in the affirmative regarding having a permanent homosexual partner in the separated group is very high: 26 per cent of the controls report they currently have a regular homosexual partner. Thus a regular partnership could be a compensation for those who have been married, in terms of an alternative way of dealing with a need for stability. Equally plausible, however, is the possibility that the ability to sustain a partnership is a positive transfer from the marriage partnership. But, comparing results with those of the control sample, it is clearly not a function of opportunities.

There was a statistical trend for the still married group to answer in the negative to the question 'Have you ever had a regular homosexual partner?' The majority of both groups, formerly and still married, answered in the affirmative, 95 per cent and 67 per cent respectively. When the degree of involvement in the homosexual subculture is looked at later, it will become apparent that this result is a function of opportunities for involvement. For those respondents who answered yes, response on the question 'If yes, was this after marriage?' was almost identical between the two groups. Nor were there any differences between the groups on the number who had had female partners apart from their wives (nearly a quarter of the married respondents had). Again, the same proportion in each group had had relationships with other women before, as against after, marriage. Such a relatively small total proportion emphasises that the majority of the married groups were predominantly homosexual in inclination. It appears that opportunity is equal over situations and groups for heterosexual relationships, but that some variations in homosexual relationships reflect both opportunities and needs of the two groups of married respondents.

Psychological adjustment, homosexual social situation, heterosexual social situation: a comparison between the two marriage groups

On the scales measuring psychological adjustment, several composite scales computed from a number of individual questions (Appendix 2) discriminated between the married but now separated and the still married and living with spouse respondents, often in cases where the individual items failed to discriminate between groups at the significance levels set. Since those individual items which do reach statistical significance can stand in their own right as well as scale items, they are discussed individually first.

Three items from the self-acceptance scale illustrated differences between the two groups of the married sample: Q37(1): 'I feel that I have a number of good qualities', Q37(19): 'All in all, I'm inclined to feel I'm a failure' and Q37(56): 'I feel I do not have much to be proud of.' In all these, the still married group were less inclined to view themselves as having good qualities, being successful and having anything to be proud of. This lower level of self-acceptance, while not reflected in the computed self-acceptance scale, does illustrate a tendency for those homosexual men still married to have a lower level of self-acceptance, which may be seen as a reason for remaining married on two bases. With lower self-acceptance homosexuality is more likely to be viewed as unacceptable and those married are also likely to need the socially acceptable institution to bolster their self-acceptance. It is quite possible that homosexuality as such may be a factor in the low self-acceptance and that acceptance of homosexuality, as is more evident in those who are no longer married, leads to rejection of marriage and an acceptance of a homosexual life-style. On the other hand, it is also possible, although much less likely, that those who have separated have been able to come to terms with their sexual orientation better in the 6.7 years on average they have been separated.

One item from the computed scale of 'interpersonal awkwardness' differentiates between the two groups: Q37 (22), 'I have a harder time than others in gaining friends.' Still married respondents answered in the affirmative more often than the separated respondents. Since none of the six items of this scale reached significance, it is more likely that this is simply a reflection of the actual difficulties in getting to know people when one is married and settled down, rather than an indication of interpersonal awkwardness.

On the depression scale, one item, Q37(46), 'I often feel downcast and dejected', was answered in the affirmative direction more often by still married than by separated respondents. This is reflected in the trend for differences between both groups on the composite depression scale to exist. This evidence that depression is a function of the marriage situation, arising from conflict between pre- ferred and actual orientation and relationship, suggests that there is, as expected, a price to pay in terms of a trend of increased depression for some homosexual men who remain married.

While the composite scale of 'conception of homosexuality as normal' shows no differences between the two groups, one item shows a significant trend: 'It would not bother me if I had children who were homosexual.' The trend is for still married respondents to indicate more worry than formerly married respondents. Since the total scale shows that both groups tend to regard homosexuality as 'normal', it seems easier to account for this result by suggesting that those who are still married are more committed to the heterosexual model of 'normality', that is, marrying and having a family, and their agreement with the statement could be a virtual admission that their whole heterosexual life-style had been unnecessary, there was nothing to react to. It can also be implied that the still married respondents would not want their children to go through the same process as themselves. On the scale of 'conception of responsibility for homo- sexuality', there is a trend for separated respondents to feel more responsible for their homosexuality than those still married. Q37(45), 'A person is born homosexual or hetero- sexual', significantly differentiates between groups, with separated respondents disagreeing more than those still married. Although not significant, trends on the two other items in the scale are in the same direction. It is interesting to note that on this measure the still married group seem to tend towards external control, the formerly married group to internal control, concepts suggested by Rotter (1966). In line with this, the internally controlled respondents could be expected to see their own behaviour as controlling the marriage situation and consequently to have expressed them- selves more than the externals would have by becoming separated or divorced.

There were three other items which were statistically significant in differentiating the two groups but which were not a part of any scale: Q37(6), 'What consenting adults do in private is nobody's business as long as they don't hurt other people'; Q37(44), 'There is nothing immoral about being a homosexual' and Q37(52), 'I would not mind being seen in public with a person who has the reputation (among heterosexuals) of being homosexual.' For the first two statements, separated individuals tend to agree more than still married respondents. Both statements appear to emphasise 'liberal' attitudes of acceptance of homosexuality. Those still married appeared to accept these statements less, in the direction expected from the differences on the self-acceptance scale items earlier. These two results confirm the hypothesis that those still married tend to accept their homosexuality less, with the result that, in some cases, they would not consider a homosexual life-style as an alternative to marriage, unlike those who have separated. The last statement is directly related to passing as heterosexual: again, as hypothesised, still married respondents were higher on 'passing' as heterosexual than separated respondents, a finding which was borne out by the differences between groups on the 'passing' scale discussed later.

A number of other items from computed scales differentiate between the two groups of the married sample. Of the scale 'being known about (by others)', the items in response to the instruction 'Check how many know or suspect you are homosexual: heterosexuals who you know, male heterosexual friends, female heterosexual friends, neighbours and people you suspect or know are homosexual' are all statistically significant in differentiating the groups. Those items not significant were, without exception, scored by both groups in the direction of not being known about. While this reflects the trend of separated respondents being better known about than still married ones (discussed below), it is interesting to note that the still married group are less known about by people they suspect or know are homosexual. This is probably indicative of much lower involvement in the homosexual subculture and less readiness to be open themselves about their homosexuality even to homosexuals, an area where it might be assumed there was little risk of rejection. The significance of the differences between groups can probably best be explained as, in this case, situational: those respondents still married have much more to lose than those separated if they are known about. There is, however, the alternative possibility that, by remaining married, they are indicating less acceptance of a homosexual life-style than those who have given up their marriages. That this may be a factor in some of the differences within the married sample is indicated by a trend on the 'anxiety regarding homosexuality' scale discussed below. Nevertheless, the trend on this scale could also be regarded as being due to situational factors.

Similar results to those obtained on the scale items of 'being known about (by others)' are obtained in the scale items of 'being known about (by family)', which asks similar questions about family and people with whom the respondent is likely to have a close relationship. To the same question 'How many suspect or know you are homosexual?', significant differences between groups were obtained for the items mother, brothers, best heterosexual friend (same sex), best heterosexual friend (opposite sex) and employer. Again, where there were no significant differences, both groups of respondents tended to be close to the end of the scale of not being known about.

The interesting point of this particular group of results is that they provide a basis, albeit small, for examining family ties and differences between groups. In this particular sample of married homosexuals, it appears that those still married feel closer to their mothers and brothers than the separated group and are more able to confide in them. Highly significant differences appear between the samples on whether best heterosexual friends (same sex and opposite sex) suspect or know of the respondent's sexual orientation. This would appear to some extent to be a situational factor, as often a person's best friends may be also good friends of the spouse. However, when considering the response of still married respondents to the item referring to people one suspected or knew were homosexual, it seems apparent that, even when there is little reason for suspicion or rejection, they tend to be more secretive and confide in fewer people than their separated contemporaries. This is borne out by reference to the individual items of the scale 'expected social reaction', where the responses to the same individuals (mother, brothers, best heterosexual friend [same and opposite sex] and most other heterosexual friends) all show significant differences between groups in the same direction.

The differences between groups would appear to be a function of those still married expecting greater rejection from the particular persons referred to, resulting in their confiding less in these particular members of their circle. There is some minor tendency, reflected in items in the computed scale 'dependence on others', for separated respondents to rely more on their immediate family than those still married, as evidenced by their considering brothers and aunts and uncles, as more important to themselves. Of the four items relating to labelling experiences, only one showed differences between the groups: separated respondents reported more problems on jobs they had had because of suspicion of their homosexuality. In view of this, it is surprising that still married respondents did not score more highly than they did on anticipated reactions of others to their homosexuality if it became known, as from this result they would seem to have had more reason to expect problems and some degree of rejection.

Further confirming the evidence that still married respondents were more concerned about exposure of their orientation is the result obtained on Q56, 'Does or would being labelled a homosexual bother you?' As expected, it would bother them more than the formerly married group. In explanation of this, still married respondents tend to answer Q58, 'Are people likely to break off a relationship with someone they suspect is homosexual?' in the affirmative more than those who were separated.

Major differences between the two groups also occur in the area of relationships with the homosexual world, as hypothesised. Two items on the scale measuring social interactions with homosexuals differentiate between the groups at a highly significant level, on proportion of leisure time spent socialising with homosexuals and proportion of homosexual friends. As hypothesised, still married respondents spend little time with, and have few friends who are homosexual

61

compared to the formerly married group. The three items comprising the scale of 'present homosexual social situation' are also significant in differentiating groups on the factors measuring how long respondents have had mostly homosexuals as friends, how well known they are amongst homosexuals and how often they frequent homosexual bars and clubs. Differences are all in the expected direction, with the still married group having less contact and being less known. Related to the last item is a measure of acculturation to the homosexual subculture, 'How often have you danced with another male?' Again, findings on the earlier item are confirmed by highly significant differences in the expected direction. The two factors discussed earlier, differences attributable to situational factors (marriage or separation) and differences attributable to greater secrecy on the part of those remaining married, again appear to be the major factors explaining these differences.

A central factor which might reinforce the latter explanations is contained in the item (Q38), 'Do you experience shame, guilt or anxiety after homosexual sex?' Differences between groups are highly statistically significant. While it is equally possible to suggest that the still married group's greater experience of guilt, shame or anxiety is a cause or result of remaining married, scores on the scale of 'expected social and peer reaction' tend to strongly suggest that this could be seen as a causal factor in marriage. Significant statistically, this scale demonstrates that still married respondents perceive the reaction of both those around and close to them and of society in general, as more condemning of homosexuality in general and of homosexual individuals. This confirms earlier suggestions that, while the still married homosexual man is more likely to remain married because of his greater conformity to current standards, including marriage, possibly for religious reasons, he is also likely to remain married because the alternative of accepting, to some extent, a homosexual life-style is unacceptable to him in the light of his own perceptions of pressures against homosexuality in the community and amongst his family and associates. Q80, 'Do you worry about possible exposure of your homosexuality?' shows significant differences between the groups, with the still married group worrying more, again a confirmation that continuing marriage may be, to some extent, a protection against the perceived wrath of society, family and friends.

The two hypotheses that being married and a homosexual will produce situational problems and less psychological well-being, and that those remaining married will be less well known about, are confirmed by the computed scales. On the scale of depression, still married respondents tend to score higher (that is, are more likely to suffer from depression) than separated respondents, presumably purely as a function of the marriage situation. There is also a trend for those still married to be more anxious about their homosexuality as measured by the scale 'anxiety regarding homosexuality' than those separated. This helps explain why such respondents remain married, although the non-affective benefits of marriage discussed earlier must also be a significant factor. Surprisingly, there is also a trend for those still married to score as more lonely than those separated on the 'loneliness' scale; probably this measures the emotional gap caused by lack of a homosexual relationship in many cases, rather than simple lack of companionship.

The three related scales of 'passing as heterosexual', 'being known about (by others)' and 'being known about (by family)' all show significant differences between the two groups. This confirms the hypotheses that still married homosexuals will be less known about and would pass as heterosexual more often. Again, this result is probably situational: those still married tend to be less known about and to pass more because of their current situation as a married person with family and all the roles associated with this, including a desire to protect their family. However, there is some degree of greater concern about homosexuality and social reaction to it involved also: the statistically significant results on the scale of 'expected reaction', together with the trends on the scales of 'anxiety regarding homosexuality' and 'conception of responsibility for homosexuality' indicate that the tendency to greater conservatism of those remaining married may play a part in the significant differences between groups on the scales measuring 'being known about' and 'passing as heterosexual'.

While there are no differences on the computed scale of 'psychosomatic symptoms', three items (Q88 [2, 12, 13]) differentiate the two groups. Most surprising, however, are the results of the items questioning psychiatric experience. The formerly married group report visiting a psychiatrist over their homosexuality more, have received more psychiatric treatment and have had more psychiatric treatment for reasons other than their homosexuality. Two factors could be implicated in this: first, those now separated probably had more problems with their marriages, consequently leading to psychiatric consultation and marriage breakup. Second, as evidenced by higher non-homosexually caused consultation, they are more likely to be open enough to see a psychiatrist about a problem, whereas to those still married, psychiatric consultation may have connotations of social unacceptability. However, the most logical explanation is that those still married find less difficulties in their marriage and whatever difficulties occur, whether homosexual or not, can be coped with. This explanation tends to confirm the earlier suggestion that still married respondents tend to have greater maturity and ability to make marriages 'work' and to benefit from the non-affective side of the partnership.

The picture that emerges from the comparison between the separated and still married homosexuals is one of some tendencies to differ. Those still married appear to be more able to cope with marriage and any conflict that may arise, but, compared to those separated, also tend to be more open to social pressure. However, in this comparison, differences shown are predominantly situational: the results reflect the results of marriage, rather than anything necessarily personality-based, in the type of person who may get married, which is more apparent in the comparison between the never married controls and the total married sample. However, there is some evidence to differentiate on this basis those who remain married, although it is not clear to what degree situational and personality-based characteristics operate. What does become clear, however, is that many of the problems one would expect to see as a function of the combination of heterosexual marriage and homosexuality are not readily apparent: instead, it can be demonstrated that these may be negated in terms of individual adaptation and adjustment, or have not in fact been problems.

In summary, it appears that the negative effects of being married and homosexual are largely confined to a slightly higher degree of depression. However, it may well be the case that those most able to cope with the situation are those who remain married and that those for whom the situation is more difficult to cope with are the individuals who separate.

6 The homosexual who marries

A second major question which may be asked in relation to marriage in homosexual men relates to the type of homosexual man who is likely to marry. In the previous chapter it was apparent that there was not a great degree of difference between those men who separated and those who remained married, which could not be explained by actually being in a marriage. In order to examine the type of homosexual who marries, it is necessary to look at the combined group of forty-two respondents who have at some time been married or are still married (the still married and the separated samples) as against the control sample (homosexuals who have never been married). The control sample was matched with the total married sample on age and educational level and, as a consequence, there are no significant differences in these variables between samples.

Analysis of variables and scales by sample (married sample and unmarried sample) yields an indication of the influence of variables on the type of respondent in the two samples. Whereas analysis of marriage situation showed the effects of marriage and, to a less extent, some personality differences between those who were married and those separated, analysis by sample should show such personality-based differences with minimal situationally based differences: these latter can be noted by reference to differences between marriage groups reported in the previous chapter. If most of the variance is accountable for in one or other marriage situation rather than between samples, then the differences obtained may be primarily a function of situation, rather than of the type of homosexual who gets married.

The biographical variables differentiate the two samples: present residence, teenage residence and type of residence. The first and last variables are also significant within the married sample, so some of the variance can be accounted for by this. Nevertheless, the differences indicate that those respondents who have married tended to come from the country or smaller towns more often than the unmarried sample. As with present residence, which is similarly significant, this is taken as one indication of greater conservatism in background and environment. It is axiomatic that rural areas and country towns exhibit a somewhat lower level of toleration of 'deviant' activity of any type and that any forces which may account for liberal views tend to occur more in larger urban areas as a general proposition. There also occurs a significant difference between samples on type of present residence, with the unmarried sample tending to live in 'Gay' flats more than the married sample, a fact which is expected and could be accounted for primarily by situation.

Four individual items of the adjustment scales differentiate between samples and reflect attitudes which are perhaps typical of the major differences on the computed scales. The married sample tended to answer negatively the question (Q37[10]), 'Most people can be trusted' compared to those unmarried respondents. This is reflected in the high significance level of the 'faith in others' scale (see Appendix 3, Table 3.2) and indicates that they have somewhat less faith in human nature and in human acceptance of homosexuality. Reflecting an aspect of this, two items from the scale 'conception of homosexuality as normal' Q37(30 and 49) showed that the married respondents see homosexuals as basically different to heterosexuals and homosexuality as having a greater negative effect on society than the unmarried respondents. This tendency to suspect the reaction of others and see those reactions, even to reflect them, as particularly repressive and anti-homosexual appears repeatedly in the married sample.

There is a strong tendency to be less known about, both by others and family in the married sample. All the items on the scale 'being known about (by others)' were significant at a higher level than the same scale's level of the significance in the comparison of groups within the total married sample in the previous chapter. Similarly, all items were significant on the scale 'being known about (by family)' at a higher level of significance than the previous comparison between the still married and separated samples. Far more than the differences between these groups, the total married sample can be differentiated very strongly from the unmarried sample as being much less known about by both people closer to them and friends and associates in general.

From this, some interesting points arise. The married sample's results tend to show significance (Appendix 3) at a much higher level for non-family female acquaintances (female heterosexual friends, best heterosexual friend [opposite sex]) than for male acquaintances. This confirms the difference on item Q37(17), that the married sample tended to find it easier to talk to male heterosexuals than female heterosexuals. With family, however, the opposite trend is apparent: the married sample tend to be known about more by female than male family members. This may suggest a closer relationship to females in the family, but some difficulty in relating to or confiding in non-family females and vice-versa with males. There is also a tendency for those people to whom the respondents in the married sample are least likely to be known, to be those from whom the strongest negative putative social reaction is expected, in terms of significance of differences between samples. It is, of course, to be expected that those from whom the worst reaction to homosexuality is expected will be those least likely to know or to be told.

All items on the scale of 'expected societal reaction' significantly differentiate between the two samples, as was expected. This is clear evidence for accepting the hypothesis that those who have married tend to anticipate a far worse general social reaction to homosexuality than those who remain unmarried: the significance level obtained was much greater than that found on items in the comparison between the two groups (still married and separated) of the total married sample, indicating that variance from that source cannot account for the magnitude of the difference. This seems clear evidence that a particular personality type of the homosexual-individual-who-tends-to-marry can be described in terms of his higher expectancy that homosexuality will be seen as unacceptable by society and by those around him. It could be further suggested that this is a factor in the marriages of many homosexuals. The whole scale seems to be summed up in the item Q40(13), 'How do you think heterosexuals in general would react to finding out that you are homosexual?' This differentiates between the married and unmarried samples at a very high level of statistical significance.

A number of other items bear on the main variable of 'expected societal reaction' and on factors which may have led the homosexual to marry. The situation at time of identification as a homosexual and around the time of marriage appears to play some part in the decision to marry. As evidenced by significant differences on two items of the scale measuring the respondent's social situation when he was identifying himself as homosexual to some degree, those who married tended to be more heterosexually socially active and to regard themselves as more popular in such circles than those who did not marry (Q45, Q47). Significant differences are also to be seen between samples on items measuring current social interaction with heterosexuals (Q44, Q48): probably as a function of passing as heterosexual and being married, there is a tendency for the married sample to report they have more contact with heterosexual circles. The responses to the question on 'passing as heterosexual' (Q51) confirm that such a relationship exists and that those who have been married try to conceal their homosexuality from more people than those unmarried at a high level of statistical significance. Reflecting the differences in heterosexual social situation are those of homosexual social situation. Similar differences are demonstrated in the items Q65 and Q66: married sample respondents tend to feel they are less popular or well known amongst homosexuals and report frequenting homosexual establishments less than the unmarried sample. Similarly, there are differences on Q70 (length of current homosexual relationship). All of these could be ascribed to current situation to a large degree and to a much lesser extent to passing as heterosexual. It is somewhat surprising to find that there is a general tendency for the total married sample respondents to feel that (Q72) most homosexuals think worse of them, compared with the unmarried respondents. Probably this is an indication that, as in Q65, it is a function of less frequent mixing in homosexual circles.

However, the major differences between samples can be grouped in the one area: as suggested earlier, there are substantial differences in areas which reflect putative societal reaction. On the scale of 'anticipated discrimination', three items are highly statistically significant: the total married sample, as contrasted with the unmarried sample, consider that people are more likely to break off a social relationship with a person who is homosexual and more likely to make life difficult for him if he is a homosexual. Additionally, they feel that they would have more problems at work if people found out about their orientation. Similarly, on the item measuring 'expected attitude towards homosexuals' (Q61) the difference in the same direction is also highly statistically significant. 'Negative expected societal reaction' is a factor which can be implicated, probably causally, in marriage of homosexual males; however, it is not necessarily an explanation in itself. Perhaps the best explanation confirmed by the data can be found in the scale measuring 'anxiety regarding homosexuality'. Of this scale, two items in particular illustrate the point, Q56 and Q82: respondents in the total married sample tended to answer in the affirmative more often that they would be more worried about being labelled homosexual and that knowing they are homosexual makes them feel guilty and ashamed, than the unmarried sample. Confirming this, married sample respondents reported significantly more often that they feel more guilty about homosexual sex than unmarried respondents and, highly significantly, that they felt more guilty, ashamed or anxious, after their first homosexual experience than those who remained unmarried. Quite clearly, as reflected in the overall scale of 'anxiety regarding homosexuality', which significantly differentiated between samples, the main variable apparent from this research which distinguishes those homosexual males who marry and those who do not marry is putative societal reaction, a major correlated component of which is anxiety about the respondent's own homosexuality. Whatever the causal relationship between these two factors, it becomes clear that the total married sample respondents' main difficulty is their tendency to 'See ourselves as others see us,' as Robbie Burns put it. By this, we are referring to the fact that their anxiety about homosexuality is projected on to society or, more probably, from society on to themselves.

Nine of the computed scales show significant differences between groups. There is a very general trend for the scale measuring 'psychosomatic symptoms to show a greater degree of psychosomatic complaints in those who are, or have been, married compared with those who have never married: five items on the scale are significant. These items include having trouble getting to sleep (early insomnia), being bothered by nervousness and feeling tense and fidgety, being bothered by headaches, having an upset stomach more frequently and tending to lose weight when something important is bothering one. It was expected that psychosomatic symptoms would be a result of situational stresses, but one cannot attribute these results to the still married group's influence within the sample, as no difference on this scale was obtained between the still married and separated samples. The most obvious conclusion is that the psychosomatic symptoms may be a function of pressures other than situational within the total married sample, as shown particularly in the large differences between samples shown on the scale 'expected societal reaction' and its associated scales, such as 'passing as heterosexual' and 'being known about (by others and family)'. Significance on these latter three scales is a little higher than for the same scales in the between-groups analysis within the total married sample. These very highly significant differences indicate that those homosexuals who are likely to marry pass as heterosexuals more often and are less known to family and acquaintances than those who remain unmarried. Such a burden of secrecy can only be reflected in psychological strain, which in turn usually appears as psychosomatic symptoms. The particularly high difference between total married and unmarried samples on 'putative societal reaction' significant at the 0.1 per cent level as compared with significance at the 1 per cent level in the between-groups analysis within the total married sample is an indicator that this reaction is probably a strong causal factor in the marriages of homosexuals. Were it situationally related to marriage rather than personality-based, it could be expected that the major differences would appear only in the between-groups analysis of the total married sample. Along with this factor, which distinguishes those homosexual men who have married, are the related factors measured by the scales of 'anxiety regarding homosexuality' and 'conception of homosexuality as normal', which differentiate the two samples in the expected direction again at a statistically significant level. It is apparent that these two measures go hand in hand and that because the total married sample see homosexuality as less normal than the unmarried sample do, they also show more anxiety about their homosexuality. The most likely explanation is that, since conception of homosexuality as normal and anxiety regarding homosexuality are products of social learning, they are learned from the perceived general social climate which is referred to as 'expected societal reaction'. However, it is not at all clear why the view of the 'expected societal reaction' to homosexuality as more unaccepting of such an orientation comes about in the married sample respondents. While the label 'personality-based' cannot explain the origin of this variable, it does express the fact that it is not a function of marriage but something which appears to be present as a predisposing factor to marriage.

The two samples can be differentiated in terms of two other scales: 'faith in others' and 'dependence on others'. In its negative form, the scale 'faith in others' appears to measure a rather generalised paranoid ideation, the extent to which people are prepared to trust others and their motives. Results indicate that the total married sample respondents show less faith in others than the unmarried controls. It is most likely that, since the married sample show a much higher unaccepting putative societal reaction, they would also have less faith in those who they feel would be so much against their sexual orientation. While the converse, that they have low faith in others and consequently feel that those others would be against their orientation, could also be true, it appears the more unlikely of the alternatives. At first glance, the higher trend towards dependence on others in the married sample would appear contradictory to this. If this sample have less faith in others and imagine society thinks their orientation is unacceptable, how can they show a greater dependence on others? However, this factor could be added to the projected reasons for marriage: it is logical, in the situation where one's orientation is felt to be unacceptable and one has a need for, or dependence on, others, that marriage should be a solution which is entirely socially acceptable and a stable other to depend on is provided.

From the analysis of the data, it is apparent that the homosexual 'type' most likely to marry can be fairly clearly differentiated from those who do not. There are some differences in background, but the major factor differentiating the two samples is the measure of 'expected societal reaction' and its associated scales measuring 'anxiety regarding homosexuality' and 'conception of homosexuality as normal'. The hypothesis that homosexual men who marry will see social reaction against homosexuality as much stronger than those who do not marry is confirmed, although the mechanism underlying this finding is not readily apparent from the background data, even though some factors are suggestive of them. Nevertheless, it is clear that those homosexual men who marry are not only more open to social pressure but see social pressure as being more threatening towards their sexual orientation as well.

In terms of the professional approach to homosexual men who have married and who seek help, it is clear that the most effective approach will probably be to minimise the expectation of negative reaction of others and society in general to homosexuality and the guilt and anxiety about a homosexual orientation. A similar approach would probably be more effective in homosexuals who indicate that they intend to marry. Acceptance of a homosexual orientation within marriage, however, is also probably likely to ultimately lead to a breakdown of the marriage. To a large extent, though, degree of homosexuality will also play a part and this is examined in the following chapter.

7 Degree of homosexuality and marriage

Bisexuality has traditionally been an area which has a number of references in the literature, but little empirical research has yet been done. The work of Kinsey, Pomeroy and Martin (1948), produced the famous Kinsey Scale on which sexual orientation was graded from complete homosexual (6), to complete heterosexual (0) on a seven point scale. In theory, any individual rating points one to five inclusive could be considered bisexual (it should be noted that the term 'bisexual' is derived from common usage: technically, it has also been used in the past to refer to persons with genitals of both sexes in the one body). The problem of definition raises a number of issues and must be considered before any attempt to empirically test hypotheses relating to bisexuality can be considered.

First, the domain of the sexual preference must be specified. Weinberg and Williams (1974) have noted that the term homosexual can be taken to refer to a number of things: inclination, activity, status, role, or self-concept. The same applies to bisexuality. Any definition could look at three discrete and possibly unrelated categories: preference (wanting to have relationships with members of both the same and opposite sexes) and self-concept (seeing oneself as having the ability to have relationships with both males and females, or defining oneself as a 'bisexual'). A further differentiation into sub-categories can be made in terms of whether these relationships are emotional, physical, or both. While it has been recognised that sex is usually the physical extension of an emotional relationship (Ross, Rogers and

74

McCulloch, 1978), the self-concept of the bisexual may be defined in terms of some six variations of category or sub-category. Thus, it may be difficult to talk of 'the bisexual' even if one defines the bisexual in terms of his (her) own self-concept, because the basis of the self-definition may differ markedly within such a selection criterion.

To further complicate the matter, there are three theories of bisexuality derived from empirical studies. It follows, of course, that the definition of the variable of bisexuality may influence the findings of research, although in the three theories outlined there has been emphasis on stated prefer-ence on the Kinsey Scale as the criterion for definition of bisexuality.

The classical approach to sexual orientation variation was that of Kinsey, Pomeroy and Martin (1948). They noted that 18 per cent of males sampled were predominantly homo-sexual for at least three years, between the ages of 16 and 55, while 4 per cent were exclusively homosexual between the same ages, and at the other end of the continuum nearly 37 per cent of males had had a homosexual experience leading to orgasm at some time, in the same age range. Two major points can be noted. First, depending on definition of the amount of homo- or heterosexual behaviour needed to classify individuals as bisexual, proportion (and number of people in one's sample and therefore sample characteristics) could vary from a third of the male population down (Churchill, 1967); second, a permanent state of bisexuality cannot be talked about if, as Kinsey *et al.* have indicated, orientation may change radically from one period in time to another. Given these data, it would seem more accurate to classify sexual orientation in terms of direction at a given point in time rather than of its history. Sexuality can thus be seen as a fluctuating variable rather than as a constant, and whether the definition of bisexual is applied to an individual could be more a matter of the time they are sampled than a steady-state variable.

In contrast to the view of Kinsey *et al.* is the view taken by Weinberg and Williams, among others, that bisexuality is a relatively steady-state variable measurable in terms of self-conception. They looked at social and psychological correlates of a bisexual self-conception in terms of seeing the bisexual as neither homo- nor heterosexual, an outsider from both groups and lacking identification with either. Their data did not confirm the bisexual as a separate entity in terms of orientation: the lack of obvious psychological problems suggested that the homosexual side was peripheral to their general existence and thus that they were not a discrete category.

A third theoretical perspective on the bisexual is that of Dannecker and Reiche (1974), who suggest that the person who classifies himself, or is classified on the basis of behaviour or preference, as a bisexual can best be described as a 'defence bisexual'. They believe that many homosexual men describe themselves as able to relate to both men and women sexually as a defence for their homosexual orientation: 'We are fairly certain that one cannot derive bisexuality from homosexuality. . . .'

Thus, given anti-homosexual social pressure, people who describe themselves as bisexual are in fact classifying themselves as not homosexual, not totally 'abnormal'. Were there no anti-homosexual pressure to push their self-rating towards the heterosexual (accepted) end of the scale, they would probably be rated as far more homosexual on the continuum. If this theory is correct, it would be expected that bisexuals (self-classification) would show more anxiety about homosexuality, see it as more abnormal and attempt to hide their orientation more than other homosexuals. These points were noted by Weinberg and Williams and support Dannecker and Reiche's hypothesis. A second test of the defence hypothesis would be to compare distributions of individuals who had some homosexual experience, on both the 'emotional preference' and the 'behavioural' Kinsey Scales: a substantial difference in proportion in each category would tend to support the suggestion that behaviour and preference are not identical. Behaviour, therefore, would be more homosexual than reported preference, in line with preference being reported as more heterosexual, as a function of social pressure.

It could be argued that the differences between groups in the married sample and between the married and unmarried samples, were due to differences in degree of homosexuality rather than in situation or type of respondent. In order to eliminate this possibility, and also to discover what influence 'bisexuality' (degree of homosexuality) has on the situation of the married homosexual and whether there is a recognisable bisexual 'type' as there is a type of homosexual who is likely to marry, analysis was carried out by the position on the 'behavioural' Kinsey Scale.

In view of Dannecker and Reiche's (1974) opinion that many homosexual men describe themselves as emotionally bisexual, or able to relate to both men and women sexually, as a 'defence' for their homosexual tendencies, analysis was not carried out by the 'emotional preference' Kinsey Scale. While the positions of individuals on both scales followed a similar pattern with positively skewed distribution (Figure 7.1), as expected from Dannecker and Reiche's work, the 'stated emotional preference' scale tended to have most respondents classifying themselves further towards the heterosexual end of the scale. It was felt that the 'behavioural' scale was less open to such bias and was consequently used as the independent variable.

As Weinberg and Williams (1974) point out, 'homosexual' (or degree of homosexuality) can refer to a number of things — inclination, activity, status, role or self-concept. The two scales selected measure activity (amount of homosexual sex) and self-concept (respondent's opinion of his degree of homosexuality) and, while minor differences were found, there was considerable agreement in terms of proportions and shape of curves.

Of course, none of the respondents could be described as bisexual in the usual sense: what is measured is the degree to which respondents are exclusively homosexual, or have had some degree of behavioural and emotional attraction to, and experience with, the opposite sex. All respondents had, in fact, identified themselves as predominantly homosexual earlier in the questionnaire. Those who reported themselves as having a relatively high degree of heterosexuality have been suggested by Dannecker and Reiche (1974) as still being homosexuals. The results obtained would thus be a function of predominant orientation rather than degrees of difference between orientations, which use of the Kinsey Scale would imply.

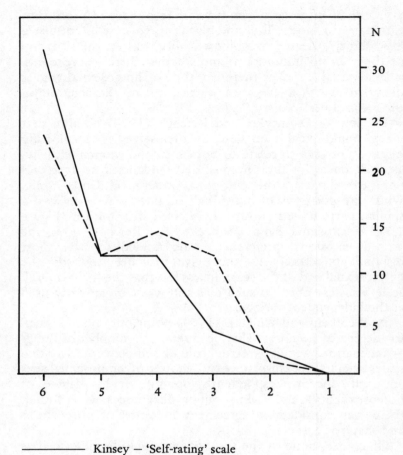

——— Kinsey — 'Self-rating' scale
- - - - - - - - - Kinsey — 'Behavioural' scale

Figure 7.1 **Position on Kinsey Scales**

A small number of variables show significant differences as a function of position on the Kinsey Scale. Obviously, marriage situation is one of these: the tendency for more of the bisexuals to marry needs no explanation. The background factor of socio-economic class also appears readily explicable, as the reason that those lower on this scale tend to report greater behavioural bisexuality is most likely a function of lower acceptance of homosexual behaviour at lower socio-economic levels. Again, as could be expected, the less homosexual respondents reported a significantly greater number of female partners other than their wife than those higher in homosexuality.

Weinberg and Williams, reporting Cory and LeRoy (1963), note that bisexuals have no particular group, neither the heterosexual world nor the homosexual subculture, with which they can identify themselves fully. This could be expected to lead to differences in psychological adjustment. These differences, however, were not apparent in their study or in the present study. However, both the Kinsey Scales, behavioural and emotional preference, can be contaminated by the attitudes of the respondent. Behaviour may well reflect the feelings of the respondent in that, if he believes homosexuality to be less acceptable than heterosexuality, he will indulge in homosexual behaviour less. Similarly, such a respondent will report himself as being less homosexual on the emotional preference Kinsey Scale as the 'defence' argument of Dannecker and Reiche suggests. No matter which scale is viewed, one cannot distinguish between genuine bisexuals and reaction or 'defence' bisexuals.

Bearing this limitation in mind, a number of interesting points about the bisexual emerge. First among these is the number of individual items of the 'self-acceptance' scale which show significant differences between the exclusively homosexual respondents and the less homosexual respondents. The less homosexual respondents disagree significantly more often with the idea that they have a number of good qualities, are people of equal worth, equal to others and have much to be proud of. While these differences are not substantiated by the overall 'self-acceptance' scale score, they suggest that the less homosexual respondents do tend to have more difficulty in accepting their orientation. Whether this is a result of those who have problems in accepting their orientation rating themselves and behaving in a less homosexual way, or bisexuals tending towards less self-acceptance in some areas, is not clear. However, since the overall 'self-acceptance' scale has not reached the level of significance indicating differences in the sample, the latter explanation would seem the more plausible. The less homosexual also tended to feel that fewer people were going to care for them (Q37[5]) and that they were born homosexual. This latter response would seem to be a good way of overcoming difficulties in self-acceptance.

Dove-tailing into the question of self-acceptance, more of the bisexual respondents cared if people knew about their homosexuality and felt that their best heterosexual friend (same sex) would be less accepting of their orientation than did the more homosexual respondents. This appears to show one difference between those with greater and lesser degrees of homosexuality, as those most worried about their orientation being found out, it will be remembered, were most concerned about their female heterosexual friends finding out. This appears to be the function of a lesser degree of heterosexuality, whereas the finding that a same-sexed friend was considered less accepting could be the function of a smaller degree of homosexuality in the respondent's total orientation balance.

The more bisexual respondents also appear to depend significantly less on their parents, both mother and father, than the more exclusively homosexual respondents. Differences also occurred in labelling experiences: being labelled homosexual would bother bisexuals more. They were also less likely to report they had had life made difficult for them because they were suspected of homosexuality. Given a lesser degree of homosexuality, these results are entirely consistent with expectations. Limiting homosexual relationships to one person is also less common with the bisexual sample, as might be again expected given a smaller homosexual component in their lives. In the computed scales, there is no evidence of any psychological problems, with the exception of the scale measuring 'anxiety regarding homosexuality', which indicated that the bisexuals were more anxious than homosexual respondents. But, as has been suggested already, this is to be expected since the bisexual would be less happy to be labelled as totally homosexual when this is only one portion of his life-style or orientation. Such a labelling would be incorrect and tend to limit his heterosexual social interaction.

Weinberg and Williams also found 'anxiety regarding homo-sexuality' as being the only scale differentiating bisexuals: they suggest that, as this does not generalise to other problems, this is evidence for compartmentalisation associated with a behaviour experienced only occasionally.

The findings of Weinberg and Williams that there are no apparent psychological problems of adjustment as a function of bisexuality are confirmed. More important, however, is the fact that none of the results obtained in comparing the married and unmarried samples, or in comparing groups within the married sample, are explained by bisexuality, or the degree of homosexuality. In fact, degree of homosexuality seems to give rise to very few differences, and even on these few measures the two Kinsey Scales are open to contamina-tion, by reflecting attitudes felt to be more socially accept-able to the respondents rather than reporting their actual behaviour unaffected by their views on its acceptability. However, it is interesting to compare 'behavioural' Kinsey Scale ratings with 'emotional preference' Kinsey Scale ratings (see Figure 7.1). If a chi-square test is computed between the numbers in each scale position by Kinsey Scale category, the result indicates that the difference is statistically significant: more individuals assessed themselves as being behaviourally exclusively homosexual than emotionally.

The implications of these findings are not exclusive in their support for the defence theory as against the other two approaches, but do suggest that the self-label of bisexual may be used as a defence of semi-acceptability for those most uncomfortable or anxious about their homosexuality. In much the same way, Townes, Ferguson and Gillam (1976) found that candidates for sex changes defined themselves as female and showed anti-homosexual tendencies. The bisexual, then, may in terms of defence be in a similar category to the transsexual, who is also suggested to be reacting to social pressure and against homosexuality (see Ross, Rogers and McCulloch, 1978) by submitting to sex change in order to validate having a relationship with a same-sex partner. While the defence in both cases is quite different, the mechanisms of social pressure acting in both cases may be identical. Ross (1978) has suggested that, at

81

least in the case of the married homosexual, this may be a result of negative putative societal reaction.

It would thus appear that, in many cases, the label of bisexual reveals either defence or guilt of an individual's homosexuality or, possibly, in some cases, a slow adaptation to one's homosexuality by first defining oneself as bisexual, then as homosexual. At an adolescent level, this could well be a normal progression from a social self-definition to an individual self-definition. However, from these data it would be both premature and an overgeneralisation to apply the defence theory to all individuals who class themselves as bisexuals. MacDonald (1981), for example, has cautioned against generalising even beyond the time of data collection and it is not possible to state that bisexuality in the present sample is a defence any more than it may be possible to describe it as a measurement of transition in sexual orientation. In this regard, while MacDonald cautions us not to confuse transitory and transitional, we still cannot assess the individual's sexuality at time of marriage. As a consequence, probably the only safe conclusion is that bisexuality appears not to explain the differences between the still married, formerly married and control groups and, in and of itself, does not contribute any clear evidence as to why individuals married.

8 Time of discovery of sexual orientation

It could probably be assumed that there might be a great deal of difference between those men who discovered that they were homosexual after they had married, and those who knew their sexual preference before they married. For example, men who knew they were homosexual to some degree before they married may well have married with the view in the back of their mind that marriage may remove the homosexual component of their partner preference. In contrast, those who discovered that they were attracted to other males after they married could be expected to show less concern over their homosexuality. However, a directly opposing hypothesis might also suggest that those who discovered that they were primarily homosexual after they had married might be *more* concerned about their sexual preference, since it would be unexpected and to a degree more unwelcome and upsetting, as well as in conflict with a marital relationship entered into in good faith. Which of these two alternative hypotheses is supported by the evidence cannot be determined on logical grounds prior to looking at the evidence.

One would therefore expect there to be a number of significant differences between those married respondents who reported they knew they were homosexual to some degree before marriage ('before' group), and those who reported they discovered this after their marriage ('after' group). However, there is, on the face of it, less difference on the so-called 'personality-based' computed scales than was expected. It is quite possible, therefore, that those who reported that they were not aware of their homosexuality until after marriage were not 'consciously' aware of this. Results obtained cannot be explained in terms of differences in marriage situation, since identical percentages were recorded in each marriage situation for 'before' and 'after' groups.

Some differences in background characteristics and attitudes and reasons for marriage become apparent between the two groups on examination of the results. There is a trend for religious affiliation to differentiate between respondents, there being more Roman Catholics in the 'after' group, and more Presbyterians and Anglicans in the 'before' group. Given that the Roman Catholic church in Australia and New Zealand has a stronger attitude against homosexuality than the latter two churches, it is not surprising that any homosexual feelings may have been 'repressed', kept from awareness ('unconscious'), or simply not admitted to for a longer time. There is also a trend for the 'before' group to report that their parents more often lived in the same city than for the 'after' group. Possibly the presence of parents in close proximity to the respondents may have induced them to marry, even when the respondents were well aware of their orientation. Interestingly, there is a highly significant difference between groups on Q21: (Do you think you have become, as a result of marriage — more homosexual; less homosexual; about the same?). Most 'before' respondents reported they were no more and no less homosexual as a result of marriage, whereas most 'after' respondents reported that they had become more homosexual as a result of marriage. It would appear that it was not until the 'after' group respondent was placed in a situation in which his sexuality had to become operative that he examined his orientation or had it made clear to him that he was to some extent homosexual, and that 'repressed' or subliminal feelings appeared at a conscious level. Consequently, one might hypothesise that the forced-choice situation of marriage makes the respondent 'more homosexual', at least at a conscious level.

As might be expected, there is a tendency for those in the 'after' group to have more children, probably as the outcome of longer period of marriage before their orientation manifested itself.

Reasons given for marriage provide some insights into the two groups. Both gave as the most important reason (the first rank) that they were 'in love'. The reason ranked second, however, differentiates the two, with the 'before' group reporting they 'thought their homosexuality would go' compared to the 'after' group's report that 'it seemed the natural thing'. Ranking third for the 'before' respondents was 'wife was pregnant'; for 'after' respondents 'pressure from girlfriend'. It is interesting to note that in both groups the third reason involves some coercion. For the 'before' group, the second reason given qualifies the first; while some married to get rid of their homosexuality, it would seem they were 'in love' in the sense that they wanted to be in love as this was a necessary part of fitting into the social stereotype and marrying. Of course, there may be those who genuinely were, or thought they were, in love. It would, however, be hard to reconcile this in the case of those respondents who report that they realised they were predominantly homosexual before marriage and were also 'in love' heterosexually. With the 'after' group, on the other hand, the first reason is explained by the second, that 'it seemed the natural thing': consciously, being in love and marrying was the natural and socially 'normal' thing to do, and unquestioned. Nevertheless, it would still appear that there was not a strong realisation of the strength of their homosexuality in the 'before' group, and that this may account for some of the apparent similarities between groups

The distinctions between groups is followed in the question 'What were the best things about marriage?' To the 'before' group, in rank order they were companionship, and children; to the 'after' group they came in reverse order. Having children is probably one of the more socially 'usual' reasons for marriage, whereas companionship, with possibly less emphasis on physical sex, could be described as a defence against loneliness, possibly, providing a stability not at that stage expected by the respondents in homosexual relationships.

Listed amongst the worst things about marriage, the 'before' group ranked first 'loss of freedom'; the 'after' group 'sex'. Again, this probably reflects the different perceptions of the respondents on becoming married: while the 'before' group were probably resigned to sex or felt they could cope with it, the realisation of their orientation left the 'after' group unprepared and transfixed in a situation which had not been envisaged. These factors were reversed in the second ranking: the 'before' group ranked second equal worst with sex 'leading a double life' and 'having to stay home'. There would appear to be a connection between the last two, the respondents wanting, or needing, to lead a double life, and yet having to stay at home. For the 'after' group, 'loss of freedom' and 'having to stay at home' were ranked second and third respectively. In terms of adjustment, it would appear that, in the married sample, having a homosexual outlet is one of the major forms of coping, although of course the sampling method could predispose to obtaining such a response set.

The 'after' group respondents indicated, as might be expected from Q21, that their homosexuality had become more important to them at some stage of marriage, presumably when they discovered their orientation. The response to the question 'Why?' supports the suggestion that 'after' group respondents may in some cases have had some awareness of their homosexuality at a fairly early stage of marriage. Ranked first was the reason 'You couldn't keep your homosexual feelings at bay', and second 'Meeting a particular Gay person'.

Strangely, the 'after' group respondents were significantly more likely to have considered remarriage if separated than 'before' group respondents. Possibly this is a further indicator of social conformity, which would help explain why there are no significant differences between groups on the scale measuring 'expected societal reaction to homosexuality'. It may well be that, if marriage of homosexuals took place as a function, amongst other things, of a perceived societal reaction against homosexuality, then those who became aware of their orientation after marriage would have a significantly less negative 'expected societal reaction' to homosexuality than those who were aware of their orientation before marriage. Since this is not the case then one must either assume that the 'after' group respondents were also reacting to perceived societal pressure and suppressing their homosexual tendencies, or suggest that the 'after' group respondents felt greater guilt on finding themselves to be both homosexual and married, especially guilty over the marriage, and that such a guilt could result in a generalising or projecting of the feeling to a perceived societal reaction unfavourable to homosexuality. However, this latter hypothesis does not explain why more 'after' than 'before' group respondents would want to remarry.

It is of interest to note that the 'after' group respondents believe that formal religion and traditional morality are both significantly more important to them than the 'before' group respondents do. At the same high level of significance the 'before' group had their first sexual experience with a woman much later than did the other group. This greater familiarity of the 'after' group with the opposite sex comes out in the significant difference between groups on Q37(36) in which the 'after' group state that they feel closer to a heterosexual of their own class than a homosexual of a lower class than do the 'before' group, who similarly report fewer heterosexual friends than the 'after' group. One could hypothesise either a greater fear of women in the 'before' group, or more probably, greater heterosexual identification in the 'after' group as explaining these findings. Such a difference appears also at the time respondents were defining themselves as homosexual, when those who were already married judged themselves to be significantly more popular in heterosexual circles than those who had discovered their orientation before marriage.

However, there are surprisingly few differences between groups on the scales of 'being known about' (by 'others' and by 'family'). The 'before' group respondents were better known to people whom they suspected or knew to be homosexual. This would appear to be a function of the fact that respondents in this group have thought of themselves as homosexual for significantly longer than the 'after' group respondents, according to their responses to Q87: 'For how long have you thought of yourself as being homosexual (or partly homosexual)?' Some small differences also occurred in public labelling experience in which 'after' group respondents, compared with the other respondents, felt more strongly that life had been made more difficult for them because someone suspected they were homosexual.

In terms of psychiatric experience, a significantly greater percentage of the 'after' group had received psychiatric treatment for their homosexuality than the 'before' group. Given that in the 'before' group many respondents may have married to cover their orientation, it is to be expected that they would not put themselves in a situation in which they could be thought to be homosexual as much as the 'after' group. Furthermore, it is also to be expected that, on finding out in the marriage situation that they were homosexual, more respondents in the 'after' group would seek psychiatric assistance regarding their orientation.

One point of interest, suggesting that for some the experience of marriage has been beneficial, is that not only do 'after' group respondents report a greater proportion of more or less exclusive homosexual relationships, but also such relationships last longer than those for the 'before' group.

Only three of the computed scales achieved significance. The measure of 'stability of self-concept' tended to differentiate between the groups showing the 'before' respondents to have less stability of self-concept than 'after' respondents. This fits in well with the picture of the respondent who married after he became aware of his homosexuality. It might be expected that a person whose opinion of himself changed from day to day would be uncertain enough at any particular time to enter into marriage, and possibly uncertain enough of his orientation and his attitude to it to think that marriage was a viable possibility. A difference is also found between groups on the scale measuring 'dependence on others', with the 'after' group depending more on others than the 'before' group. It is possible that this is a function of marriage and learning a more complete dependence on another, which the 'before' respondents may not have been able to do so easily, already being aware that their allegiance lay in other areas to some extent. However, it is also possible that these people were more dependent initially. As expected, 'before' group respondents are better known about as homosexual by their family than 'after' group respondents. Given greater dependence on others and no differences in perception of societal reaction within the total married sample ('before' and 'after' groups) it is quite consistent that people who depend more on others would not let those others closest to them become aware of something to which they are expected to be antagonistic.

Overall, the general lack of differences between the two groups of respondents who were aware of their homosexuality before marriage and those who report becoming aware of their orientation after marriage, are somewhat surprising. One would have expected on logical grounds more drastic consequences of this discovery to be apparent in the 'after' group, and the factors which have strongly differentiated the married sample from the unmarried sample, particularly 'expected peer and societal reaction to homosexuality', not to be so readily apparent in the 'after' group respondents, leading to significant differences between groups. That scores on 'expected social reaction' are equally high in both groups suggests that, without being aware of the situation, the 'after' group respondents may have been acting against their orientation until, in the forced-choice situation of marriage, the repression could no longer function. In the reasons and attitudes given regarding marriage this tends to be borne out, confirming also the hypothesis that many of the 'before' group married as a reaction from their homosexuality. All in all, no general distinctions can be made between the groups: one could perhaps make a tentative suggestion that 'reaction' and 'repression' are not far removed from one another, particularly when one considers the similarities between these groups as measured and the considerable differences obtained on the same measures between the total married, and unmarried, samples.

In summary, then, it would appear that those individuals who know they were to some degree homosexual prior to marriage did tend to marry in order to de-emphasise their homosexuality. On the other hand, it does appear that those whose homosexuality became obvious after their marriage may well have had some awareness of their sexual preference subconsciously, but that it was not thrust into importance until after marriage and recognised for what it was. The differences between these two groups would appear to be in terms of their thinking about their sexuality and the levels of that thinking before marriage, rather than in terms of the different effects discovery of sexual preference before or after marriage. In terms of these effects, the two groups are remarkably similar, and it can probably be concluded that discovering one's sexual direction after marriage does not lead to any great trauma compared with knowing something about one's sexual preference prior to marriage.

9 Time of wife's discovery of husband's orientation

What effect does the wife of the homosexual man have on his adjustment and adaption? It might be expected that those men whose wives knew of their sexual preference prior to marriage would be better adjusted, and that those who never let their wives know of their homosexuality might show strain as a result of having to hide things from their spouses.

Breakdown of the data by the time of the wife's discovery, or her being informed, of her husband's homosexuality ('before' marriage, 'after', or 'never') yields a picture of the type and attitudes of the person who enters into marriage with openness about his orientation and adaptations, the problems and adjustment difficulties faced by those who must adapt after marriage has been entered into, and the way those who keep the knowledge of their homosexuality from their wives adapt to the so-called 'double-life style' and any strains this may lead to. In some cases, where the 'before' and 'after' groups show near-identical levels on a particular item and the 'never' group show a significantly different level from the other two groups, it would seem reasonable to assume that the difference is due to the 'double-life' strains which are hypothesised to occur in the 'never' group respondents.

Differences in this series of analyses are not due to differences in marriage situation, since there is a very even spread of the three groups currently under analysis over the two marriage situations (still married and separated), although with a slight trend for the 'never' group respondents to be still married. Nor are they due to differences in whether or not the respondents themselves knew before or after marriage of their orientation, since again the percentages in each group are fairly evenly spread throughout each of the three categories, although, of course, there were no figures in the cell with regard to those who found out about their orientation after marriage and those who told their wives before marriage. The pattern appears to be that, at the time of the study, around two-thirds of the respondents had told their spouses, either before or after marriage, and one-third had never told them.

There were no significant differences on background characteristics between the groups. However, on the Kinsey Scale (self-report) there was a trend for those respondents who considered themselves most homosexual to have told their spouses earlier. It was also apparent that respondents in the 'never' group had significantly more children than those in the other two groups. This could well be a factor inhibiting their telling their wives of their orientation, since any resulting difficulties in the marriage could be felt to damage the children.

A difference between groups can be seen by looking at the reasons given for each group for getting married. Before group respondents ranked as the most important reason for marriage 'pressure from girlfriend', whereas the other two groups ranked first 'being in love', second that they 'thought their homosexuality would go'. It seems clear that a fair proportion of those who told their wives before marriage were not the instigators of the union, and that those respondents who told their wives after marriage, or never, were hoping that they could condition themselves to heterosexuality through practice, and that their orientation would be changed by conforming to the common practice of falling in love and having children. This latter reason, and 'it seemed the natural thing', were the third-ranked reasons for the 'never' and 'after' groups respectively. These contrast with the second reason given by the 'before' group, that 'the spouse was pregnant'. The picture emerges of the 'before' group being pressured into marriage in spite of their orientation, and the other respondents believing, in all probability quite genuinely, that conformity to the norm would lead to the cessation of the problem, or at least its disappearance from view.

Such a dichotomy between the 'before' group and the 'after' and 'never' groups can again be seen in regard to the question: 'What were the best things about marriage?' While all three groups had, as the first factor, companionship, as second ranked factor the 'before' group respondents listed 'someone to talk to', while the other two groups reported 'children' to be the second-best thing about marriage. Again, these differences help to indicate the two clusters of respondents and their differing outlook on marriage, those in the 'before' group emphasising the more conventional and accepted aspect of marriage, children, with its implied emphasis on conjugal sex.

Of the factors considered the worst thing about marriage, 'the loss of freedom' and 'having to lead a double life' were stressed by both the 'before' and 'after' groups, while, in addition, the 'never' group respondents considered 'sex' equally bad. While two-thirds of the total married sample had spouses who were aware of their husband's orientation, it is clear that having to lead a double life and have homosexual relations without their wife's knowledge is a reasonably common adaption. This was confirmed in interviews with the sample.

Q27 ('Did your homosexuality become increasingly important to you at any stage of marriage?') gives an indication of one of the reasons why respondents in the 'after' group told their wives of their orientation. These respondents report that significantly more than either of the other two groups, their homosexuality became more important to them at some stage of marriage. Along with the 'never' group, they give as the reason for this the fact that they 'couldn't keep their homosexual feelings at bay'. When we consider the scale measuring 'expected social reaction to homosexuality', it becomes apparent that, while both these groups experienced problems in this regard, only those with the lower 'expected societal reaction' score were able to tell their wives of their difficulties. In contrast, 'before' group respondents who reported that their orientation became more important to them in marriage indicate that this was primarily a function of the marriage situation and problems arising from it.

Indications of the greater fear of being exposed as homosexual of the 'never' group, and, to a considerably lesser extent of the 'after' group, as compared with the 'before' group, are common throughout the analysis. On question 37(21) 'I do not care who knows about my homosexuality', the 'after' and 'never' groups disagree most, and similarly in regard to the statement 'People have made fun of me because I am homosexual', 'before' group respondents agree more than respondents in the two other groups. Similarly, the individual items of the scales of 'being known about' (by 'others' and by 'family'), all items are significant with the pattern being that the 'before' group were less worried than the 'after' group, who were less worried than 'never' group respondents, about being known as homosexual. An exception exists, however, with regard to the items 'people you suspect or know are homosexual' (no difference between groups, all reasonably well-known) and 'neighbours' (no difference, none well-known). It is quite likely that, as well as being indicative of 'expected societal reaction to homosexuality' differences, the 'before' less than 'after' less than 'never' pattern may reflect differences in the length of time the particular respondents in these groups have been known as homosexuals or open about their homosexuality to themselves and others, with the same relationship applying. Thus it would be expected that those who had been 'open' for a longer period of time would also tend to be known better and those who were not open were not well known about, as measured by these two scales. However, as regards the items on the scale measuring 'expected societal reaction to homosexuality', again all individual items on the scale showed significant differences between groups with the exception of mother (all groups reporting similarly moderate anticipated reaction) and brothers, neighbours, and heterosexuals in general (all consistently anti-homosexual anticipated reaction). The pattern in the total scale, apart from these exceptions, was one of 'before' and 'after' groups being generally very similar, and 'never' group considerably higher, in anticipating societal reaction of strong anti-homosexuality.

In line with this, on Q51 the 'never' group indicate they would try to hide their homosexuality from almost everyone, whereas the 'before' group, and to a slightly lesser extent the 'after' group, would not attempt to hide it from such a great proportion of people. Since passing as heterosexual is apparently a function to a large extent of anticipated discrimination, it comes as no surprise that an identical pattern manifests itself in regard to Q53, in which 'never' group respondents anticipate a greater amount of discrimination than the other two groups. As would be expected from the lower profile of the 'after' and 'never' group respondents with regard to their orientation, and also considering the time element mentioned above, the pattern of 'before' greater than 'after' greater than 'never' with regard to frequency of being labelled as homosexual significantly differentiates the two groups. Similarly, this pattern holds for reports of life being made difficult for the respondents as a result of their being suspected as homosexual. With greater and longer openness, 'before' group respondents report greater acculturation to the homosexual subculture.

In the field of psychiatric experience, the above pattern again operates, with 'before' group respondents having it suggested to them that they receive psychiatric treatment for their orientation more than 'after' group respondents, who, again, have this suggested to them more than 'never' group respondents. This is clearly reflected in the proportion in each group who have actually visited a psychiatrist regarding their homosexuality. It would be expected that those who kept their orientation the most hidden would have felt it to be the most undesirable behaviour and to have had the most psychological problems regarding marriage-homosexuality problems, and thus had more need to visit a psychiatrist. But this appears not to be the case: those who are most open about their homosexuality are most likely to reveal this to their psychiatrist, or equally possible, conversely, the psychiatrist helped them to be more open about their orientation. There was unfortunately no question asked which would indicate at what stage the respondents saw a psychiatrist: interviews with the sample suggest that it was usually either prior to marriage or when a marriage was under strain.

Nevertheless, it is quite possible that the 'never' group respondents are those who have adapted better, and not had any need to inform their wives. In this connection, it is interesting to note that 'never' group respondents tend to depend significantly more on their heterosexual friends, and this may be a factor which makes it unnecessary to confide in others. However, if such difference does exist to any degree, it is not reflected in the computed variables.

Five computed variables differentiate significantly between the three groups. On all these variables bar one the familiar pattern 'before' less than 'after' less than 'never' is repeated. The scale measuring 'obviousness of homosexuality' (as measured by amount of reported public behaviour conforming to the homosexual stereotype) shows the more obvious are those who are least worried about being homosexual. This is in direct reversal of what is found in the scale measuring 'passing as heterosexual', where significant differences show the 'never' group to be highest in passing, as heterosexual the 'before' group lowest. Connected with passing as heterosexual, further significant differences of the same form are found between the three groups on the scales of 'being known about' (by 'others' and by 'family').

The main pattern, which has been found throughout the analysis of the roughly equal graduations of degree of being known about, is continued and confirmed in the computed variables. Since the factors such as marriage situation and length of time of knowledge of the respondent's own orientation are not weighted in any way so as to influence this analysis, but are more or less randomly spread, it must be concluded that the later the respondent informed his wife (or the wife found out about her spouse's homosexuality), the more concerned that respondent was about his homosexuality, and the more likely he was to have married to hide or to try to overcome his orientation.

An exception to the pattern, however, is the scale of 'expected societal reaction', which shows no great differences between the 'before' and 'after' groups and considerably and significantly higher 'expected anti-homosexual societal reaction' for the 'never' group. This finding tends to emphasise one similarity between the first two groups: both have, at the time of answering the research instrument, told their spouses and have seen, presumably, that societal and peer reaction is not as negative as might have been assumed. However, for all groups the level of expected societal and peer reaction is higher than for the never-married sample, so it can only be assumed that, for the 'after' and 'never' groups, and to a lesser extent the 'before' group, marriage was an attempt to hide or change their orientation, as is evidenced by the reasons and attitudes given for marriage. There seems to be a gradient from 'before' through 'after' to 'never' groups which indicates increasing concern with respondents keeping their homosexuality undercover, especially from their wives. However, each group seems to have found its own level of adaption, since there appear to be a few obvious psychological consequences stemming from any of the levels of the wife's knowledge of their husband's orientation.

In summary, the differences between the three groups of individuals who had at some time been married and who had told their wives before marriage that they were homosexual, after marriage, or never told them, seem to follow the same pattern. While as expected those individuals who had never told their wives about their sexual preference were more anxious about their homosexuality being known about and expected a worse societal reaction to it, they did not suffer from what has been termed a 'double life' at all. This leads one to conclude that the differences found between the groups may be a function of the degree and particularly the time they 'came out' as homosexual, and not of whether their spouse knows or when she was told. Thus the negative consequences of leading a supposedly conflicting existence are not at all obvious, and it can only be concluded that being married and having one's spouse unaware that her partner is homosexual does not lead to psychological problems.

10 Expected societal reaction and marriage

At this point, it will have become apparent that there has emerged a common thread in the variables which differentiate the married, separated and unmarried homosexual men, and those who told their spouses of their sexual preference as against those who never told them. That common thread appears to be the variable of 'expected societal reaction against homosexuality'. While theoretical aspects of societal reaction and the implications it has for mental health in homosexuals have been discussed by Ross (1978), it would appear to have considerable importance as one of the underlying variables promoting marriage in homosexual men. It is therefore central to the investigation of the married homosexual man, and its relationship to this phenomenon will be examined in this chapter.

The preceding chapters have dealt with the five analyses of the married homosexual male as a clinical entity: married versus separated, total married sample versus never married sample, bisexuals, time of discovery of sexual orientation (before versus after marriage) and time of wife's discovery of her spouse's orientation. In this section the theoretical and experimental implications of these findings are investigated in greater depth. Four general areas will be covered: societal reaction theory with regard to the study of homosexuals; the correlates of conformity to the orthodox sexual lifestyle (heterosexual marriage) as measured by the scale of 'expected peer and societal reaction'; a factor-analytic study of the research instrument; and a comparison of findings with those of other studies.

Homosexuality has been studied mainly by psychologists and psychiatrists, who have often viewed the behaviour as a psychopathological condition. Given this emphasis, the vast majority of studies have compared homosexuals with heterosexuals. Within the last few years, however, it has been noted that the only difference between homosexuals and heterosexuals, other things being equal, is the choice of sex object itself (Gagnon and Simon, 1973). The differences which were assumed to arise from the condition of homosexuality were, when investigated, not at all apparent, as Hooker (1957) commented.

Sociological study of the area of homosexuality began, in part, in order to get away from the medical model of homosexuality. It tended to rest more solidly on the emphasis that 'The patterns of adult homosexuality are consequent upon the social structures and values that surround the homosexual after he becomes or conceives himself as homosexual . . . .' (Simon and Gagnon, 1967). In this context, Weinberg and Williams (1974) have used societal reaction theory as a model to study homosexuality. This theory sees deviance as being 'defined by the evaluations and responses of people to various behaviours. . . . What makes homosexuality "deviant", according to reaction theory, is not anything about the behaviour but rather the fact that people differentiate, stigmatise and penalise alleged homosexuals' (ibid.). Weinberg and Williams, guided by societal reaction theory, studied the male homosexual in three Western societies in which homosexuality is viewed predominantly in two forms, relatively accepted and highly unaccepted. The rationale behind the comparison was that 'One might expect different consequences for the homosexual's well-being in societies that vary in their reaction . . . this is a major implication of societal reaction perspective' (Weinberg and Williams, 1974). Results of the study, however, did not confirm the expectations: no significant differences were found in the psychological well-being of subjects between the three cultures (the United States, the Netherlands and Denmark).

The lack of difference between the three cultures would seem to be due to one main factor being overlooked: that it is not purely and simply the society's reaction, but the individual's reaction to the society's reaction which leads to psychological problems. If the individual in any given society sees that society's reaction as being violently anti-homosexual, then he is likely to be more concerned or anxious about this than another individual in the same society who takes a more optimistic view. This is not to say that societal reaction has no place in the investigation of the homosexual, but that it is only a part of the conditions which must be investigated. To use an analogy, societal reaction is like a bacterium: in order to reproduce, it needs a suitable environment. While cold, dry conditions may not be very suitable, in warm, humid, food-rich conditions, such as an agar plate provides, a culture rapidly becomes established. If we see the individual, or individual differences as the environment and societal reaction as the bacteria, then it becomes apparent that a further critical field to be studied in the investigation of homosexuality is that of individual differences.

Working on this assumption, the present study has set out to determine if such a proposition can be substantiated. With societal reaction as a constant (that is, with subjects from the one society), two groups were selected, those predominantly homosexual men who had married heterosexually, and might be considered to have shown a fairly strong reaction to societal reaction against homosexuality, and predominantly homosexual men who had not married. If the assumption stated above were true, then significant differences should be found between the two groups in individually perceived (expected) societal reaction, those having married being expected to see societal reaction as more anti-homosexual than those who remained unmarried.

The data confirm the hypothesis, the difference between the two groups being highly statistically significant. The data further confirm the hypothesis by demonstrating a similar significant difference in the same direction, between those respondents who separate and become more openly homosexual and those who remain married: the more anti-homosexual the perceived reaction, the more likely the individual is to stay married and keep attempting to hide his predominant orientation.

The implications of such a finding, which may at first

sight seem a rather obvious one, are twofold. First, the psychiatrist need not study the homosexual by using the medical model, but using the social approach with concentration on the individual as well as the society, rather than the sociological societal reaction approach. In this way, the findings of more recent researchers, that the homosexual is not necessarily different from the heterosexual (Dean and Richardson, 1964; Ross, 1975), can be incorporated while still making the homosexual a valid research object. The method has again been demonstrated by the present study, using homosexuals as controls for homosexuals and examining areas where potential problems, such as homosexuals marrying, can be studied without implications of any necessary abnormality or need to abandon study of the individual for the study of his social environment. Ideally, of course, the two should proceed together.

Second, since the differences found between groups cannot be accounted for by any readily apparent background factors, or by any differences in conservatism as measured by the Wilson-Patterson Conservatism Inventory, it would seem reasonable to suggest that they result from individual differences in personality operating as situation-specific conformity. In any case, the findings do suggest that homosexuals could be a fruitful area for further research into aspects of conformity and underlying personality correlates.

Aspects of expected peer and societal reaction against homosexuality

Since expected peer and societal reaction has been implicated strongly as a personality-based factor in both those homosexuals who have married, and those who have remained married, as well as in those who have not made their wives aware of their orientation, it is necessary to examine its components in some detail. Using the same form of investigation as the five previous analyses but with the scale of 'expected peer and societal reaction against homosexuality' (ESR) as the independent variable, correlates of high ESR were examined.

Only two background factors were found to be associated

with high ESR, both associated with residence. Those who lived with their wives were higher on this scale than those living in any other place, confirming earlier findings, and those who had spent their teenage years in the country again had significantly higher scores than those who had spent them in a town or city.

Of the computed scales measuring psychological adjustment, six items were significant, four of which were from the two scales of 'self-acceptance' and 'conception of homosexuality as normal', although these scales as a whole did not reach significance. The items 'I feel I have a number of good qualities', 'At times I feel no good at all' and 'I feel able to do things as well as most people' from the former scale showed that a significant number of respondents who indicated disagreement were high on ESR. On the scale measuring 'conception of homosexuality as normal' the two highly significant items were 'homosexuality may best be described as an illness' and 'homosexuals and heterosexuals are basically different in more ways than simple sexual preference.' It is not surprising to see that those who imagine the 'generalised other', which ESR could well be described as measuring, as being anti-homosexual show to some extent lower self-acceptance of themselves as homosexuals. However, it is not possible to say whether this is causally linked. It would seem more probable that a respondent who saw societal reaction as so strongly against his life-style, and conformed to that reaction or social pressure, would have his early lack of self-acceptance confirmed. It is hard to see a person who originally had relatively high self-acceptance altering that as a result of external pressure. Similarly, associated with a low score on the 'conception of homosexuality as normal' scale, it is probably a case of confirmation of early views by perceived social pressure, although obviously this is a matter for further investigation. The final item from the psychological adjustment scales is 'I often feel downcast and dejected', which forms part of the depression measure: it is highly probable that this is a function of an anti-homosexual ESR. Such correlations of these items raises the suggestion that ESR may be in fact a selective confirmation of underlying differences in conception of homosexuality and its associated problems of self-acceptance. While it would be going too far to suggest that the respondents in this study were hearing and seeing what they wanted to hear and see in terms of societal reaction, some degree of this would appear likely.

As expected, and as would be predicted by the strong relationship noted earlier between ESR and 'being known about' (both by 'others' and by 'family), almost all items on these two scales were significantly correlated with high ESR. The two exceptions were the items 'work associates' and 'employer': since most respondents preferred people in these two categories not to know about their homosexuality, regardless of degree of ESR, such a result is not surprising. However, both exceptions showed a trend in line with the other items in the scale. Similarly, on the 'family' scale, the item 'sister' was in an almost identical position although in most cases the sister was likely to know.

All items on the ESR scale of course correlated very highly with the total scale score with the exception of the item 'wife'. This, however, was due to the fact that half the married respondents were separated, and of those remaining two-thirds of the wives knew about their husbands homosexuality.

It has been suggested earlier that ESR is associated with conformity. This suggestion is supported by the fact that those high in ESR also indicate that they think homosexuality violates conformity in general significantly more often than those low on ESR. Rather than considering whether one factor causes the other, on examination it would appear that ESR is a reflection of the so-called 'generalised other' (society and personal acquaintances) and their imagined opinions from the point of view of the respondent. This is also precisely how conformity was defined earlier (the perceived strength of a pattern of social stimuli acting upon a person, emphasising conformity to a social heritage). Consequently, there is probably some justification, not only by definition but by correlation, for considering that ESR as a scale is also a measure of 'conformity' to the orthodox sexual pattern with reference to homosexuality in this case.

Associated with high ESR (referred to synonymously as

conformity below) are a number of items which it was expected would correlate highly with conformity, as well as individual items of the scale. In the area of passing as hetero-sexual ('From how many people do you try to conceal your homosexuality?'), anticipated discrimination ('Would there be problems at work if people found out?', 'Do you thing people are likely to break off a social relationship with someone they suspect is homosexual?', 'Do you think people are likely to make life difficult for people they suspect are homosexual?') and at a highly significant level these factors are correlated. Clearly, not conformity as such but the control of resources, and thus the possession of power to control the positively reinforcing condition of tension reduction or the negatively reinforcing condition of pain or harm is the factor which accounts for this particular beha-viour, as has been suggested by Bandura, Ross and Ross (1963). Similarly Kelman (1961) has defined internalisation as accepting and making another's influence one's own because it is rewarding to do so. Thus, conformity would seem to be a clear way of maximising the positive influences of, if not society, a majority of its members. Support for this suggestion can be found in the item asking 'How do you think most people feel about homosexuals?' There was again a highly significant correlation between the view that reaction would be strongly anti-homosexual and those who scored highest on ESR. Further in line with this, such people were significantly more likely to worry about possible exposure of their homosexuality and to have felt fear and guilt after their first homosexual experience and over homo-sexual sex at present (Qs 80, 83, 84). It may not be a coinci-dence that the one item in the psychosomatic scale which is significant when compared with those who are high in conformity with regard to their homosexuality is the item 'Are you ever bothered by nightmares?' Those high on the ESR scale tend to answer strongly in the affirmative.

Some further background variables which would appear to be a function rather than a cause of high conformity with regard to homosexuality have also been isolated by this analysis. At a highly significant level, those who are high on the ESR scale have less homosexual friends, and consider themselves to be not really known amongst homosexuals. Acculturation is also significantly lower, with fewer who are high on ESR having danced with another male or have made kissing part of their homosexual practice.

On the computed scales, again the trends are as expected. At a highly significant level those who are high in conformity are also high on the scale measuring 'anxiety regarding homosexuality'. Since those who think that society is most anti-homosexual and who are themselves homosexual are most likely to be anxious about their orientation, such a finding is entirely consistent. Similarly, in view of such consistency, it is also to be expected that those high in ESR (conformity) would be highest in passing as heterosexual.

This is confirmed on the 'passing' scale at a highly significant level. Rather surprisingly, there is a trend towards a relationship between high ESR and the loneliness scale. On reflection, however, given that almost all the respondents are predominantly homosexual, it could be expected that those who are most against showing any homosexual tendencies would be those who are the most lonely. They are more likely to cut themselves off more from any homosexual emotional attachments and possibly lack the ability to emotionally relate to their wives in terms of their total personality, leaving a degree of loneliness. Such a finding is confirmed by a similar trend on the scale of 'homosexual commitment', indicating less commitment to homosexuality by those who imagine it to be more frowned upon socially.

So far, ESR and conformity have been looked upon as one factor: while for the purpose of general analysis they can be regarded as essentially the same, ESR measures the putative (or anticipated) reaction of peers and society in general to homosexuality, while conformity is the behavioural reaction to such an attitude. In the psychological literature, Sherif (1935) noted that individual norms often gave way to group norms resulting from social interactions; Asch (1952) also, in a series of classical experiments, found, in situations where social judgments were made, errors tended to go in the direction of the group norm or standard. It is in such a context that homosexuals becoming heterosexually married may be seen. Three kinds of mechanisms have been proposed (Lazarus, 1971) for such a general phenomenon as conformity: first, the possibility of rejection or disapproval by the group, which maintains power over the individual by virtue of his need for affiliation. Were this the case, in the present study greater need for affiliation would be expected in the higher-scoring respondents on the ESR scale, reflected in an associated high scoring on the 'dependence on others' scale. Such an association was not found. Second, Lazarus cites the need for confirmation of one's judgment by others; and third, a personality disposition to erect and use defences in threatening contexts between the individual and group. None of these mechanisms need be mutually exclusive. However, the data tend to support the third explanation, with conformity the mechanism or personality disposition being used as a defence for the perceived strongly anti-homosexual views of peers and society.

Lazarus went on to note that there were two possible processes which individuals in such a conflict situation could follow: either 'sticking to one's guns or knuckling under', or denial and repression. Both processes are evident in the present study, the predominant one being that of 'knuckling under' (conforming), but with the second process being evident in the group of those who reported being unaware of their homosexuality until after marriage. Those who conform, it has been noted by Breger (1963), reflect a number of defensive personality characteristics. The present data would generally support the suggestion that what Breger called 'yielding' has some clear personality characteristics associated with it, although further research to investigate the antecedents of such behavioural-report measures as 'passing as heterosexual' and 'anticipated discrimination' is obviously needed.

Conformity has long been thought to be a factor in the authoritarian make-up (Adorno *et al.*, 1950). Byrne (1974) states that the 'individual whose ideas of right and wrong are simply a function of contemporary external social pressure would be expected to be receptive to authority.' To test such an assumption, the Wilson-Patterson Inventory was included in the questionnaire: while not strictly a measure of authoritarianism, very high correlations would be expected between the F-scale (measure of authoritarianism) of Adorno *et al.*, and the Wilson-Patterson Conservatism Inventory (Wilson, 1973).

No differences of any significance, nor any trend was found between any group on all analyses on the Wilson-Patterson Conservatism scale. In the analysis in which the greatest differences would be expected to be found, that between the married and the non-married samples, the mean score for the married sample was 27.857, for the unmarried sample 26.190: less than two points difference on a hundred-point scale. The only conclusion which one could be justified in reaching with these data would be that conformity is highly situation-specific, rather than a general unitary trait. While the respondents in the present study show conformity differences with regard to their homosexuality, there is ample evidence from their conservatism scores that they are at the liberal end of the scale, and substantially lower in conservatism than the specificity in conformity, at least in the homosexual sphere, Byrne (1974) has reported that, while some studies have shown a moderately high positive correlation between conforming and authoritarianism, several others have reported negative findings.

In finding no relationship between conservatism and conformity, and in stating that homosexuals who marry heterosexually are conforming, we are suggesting two things. First, and most important, there is no overall 'conforming' personality type involved. While there may be evidence for 'yielders', this is apparently not the type of individual found as a respondent in the present study: the respondents are conformists specifically with regard to their homosexuality. Second, there is an obvious reason for this specific conformity, notably, their perception that society is particularly anti-homosexual, and there would be negatively-reinforcing consequences unless their orientation is hidden by conforming to extremes with the current socially accepted heterosexual family life-style. Other homosexuals who do not share the rather pessimistic view of the unacceptability of, and dire consequences following, a homosexual life-style do not go to such extreme lengths to hide their orientation. Clearly, then, personal involvement in a problem area such as this is not a sufficient cause for such a drive to conform: one must look to the factors which precede the 'expected peer and societal reaction to homosexuality' to determine the source of such situation-specific conformity.

There can be little doubt that, apart from individual differences in backgrounds and adaptations, the main factor implicated as important in the heterosexual marriages of predominantly homosexual men is their more anti-homosexual perception of the attitudes of their contemporaries and society, and thus the more negative consequences of living a homosexual life-style. However, such a finding of a presumably personality-based difference has little theoretical value unless any such differences can be specified: while the cause of homosexuals marrying may have been traced back one step, the present study was not designed to pursue the problem of situation-specific conformity to its more remote antecedents. Nevertheless, from a clinical point of view, such a series of findings as the present ones are encouraging, since therapeutic paths may be followed which are not such great steps of faith and intuition as previously in the counselling and understanding of the married homosexual man.

11 Married homosexuals in three societies

So far, a number of married homosexuals in one culture have been looked at in detail. However, several questions which were posed previously have yet to be answered. These questions are important further tests of the findings on expected societal reaction (ESR). If ESR is a factor related to marriage of homosexual men in a causal fashion, then one would expect to find different (higher) proportions of homosexuals who had married in societies which were more anti-homosexual than in those which were most accepting of homosexual behaviour. In addition to this, one would also expect to find higher proportions of homosexual men who were still married in the most anti-homosexual societies.

There is a second reason for attempting to look at proportions of married homosexuals in other societies, even if there are not found to be any differences in the proportions across societies. An estimate is needed of the proportions of homosexual men who have married in other societies which were cited earlier, in order to ascertain whether, when one looks at other Western societies, the proportion is similar to those previously found. This relates to the reliability of the estimates of both other researchers and of the present research.

In their study in 1974, Weinberg and Williams found significant differences in the proportion of their male homosexual respondents who had been married when compared by position on the Kinsey Scale. From Weinberg and William's tabulated data, it is possible to compute the proportions of homosexual men (Kinsey Scale levels 2 to 5 inclusive) who had been married in the three cultures they studied. These three cultures were the United States (anti-homosexual) and the Netherlands and Denmark (less anti-homosexual). The proportions of homosexual men who had at some time been married were United States, 16.93 per cent; the Netherlands, 8.48 per cent; and Denmark, 8.44 per cent. These differences in proportion are statistically significant ($\chi^2_2 = 36.11$, p<.01; calculated from Table 1, p. 213 of Weinberg and Williams [1974]).

Thus it would appear that, as hypothesised above, a greater proportion of homosexual men, at least in the three countries studied by Weinberg and Williams (1974) in 1968-70 have been married in the more anti-homosexual society (United States): the proportion who had been married is nearly double that of the Netherlands and Denmark, which have virtually identical percentages. Is social environment, particularly the anti-homosexual stance in a society, reliably reflected in the proportion of married homosexual men? If this hypothesis is correct, it might be expected that Sweden would have a rate approximately half that of Australia, with Finland between the two and probably closer to Australia. The position of Finland as more anti-homosexual than Sweden and closer to Australia (where in the two states from which the sample was derived homosexual acts were a criminal behaviour) derives from the fact that while homosexuality was legalised between consenting adults in Finland at the time of the study, it could not be discussed positively in public. An enforced law in Finland (described by Ross and Talikka, 1978 and 1979) prohibits any positive public discussion of homosexuality as 'public propagation', and as a consequence most of the information available to homosexuals degraded their sexual orientation. For this reason, it is probable that the proportion of homosexuals marrying in Finland would be closer to that in Australia, where the homosexual was stigmatised in criminal law in the two states studied although not necessarily always in public utterances as in Finland. The general argument is that the more homosexuals are stigmatised, the higher will be the proportion marrying, and staying married.

The data illustrated in Table 11.1 confirm that there is a

significant difference between the three societies in this regard, and in the expected direction. It is particularly interesting to note that the proportion of Swedish homosexual men who had married was almost half that of the Australians (7.5 per cent as against 13.5 per cent). The Finns were, as hypothesised, between the Swedes and Australians, although much closer to the Australians and only some 0.8 per cent below them. Thus it would appear that actual societal pressure against homosexuality does have a bearing on the proportion who marry heterosexually.

Table 11.1 **Number and proportion ever married**

	Married	*Never married*
Sweden	13 (7.5%	161 (92.5%)
Australia	21 (13.5%)	135 (86.5%)
Finland	18 (12.7%)	124 (87.3%)

$\chi^2_2 = 5.53$, p<.05

Given this argument, it would also be expected that such societal pressure would also be reflected in the proportions who remained married or who separated. These data are illustrated in Table 11.2, and it can be seen that on this variable also a somewhat similar pattern emerges. However, while Sweden has the lowest number still married as expected, Finland has the highest with Australia in the middle position. While it is not appropriate to go into detail with such small samples, it would appear that societal reaction does have some effect on the continuation of marriage or separation. There would, however, be a very considerable personal and interpersonal dimension to making a decision about the continuation of marriage, and such a decision would also depend on the spouse and the quality of marriage, so it would not be expected that there would be an entirely socially-determined response to this variable.

On the other hand, self-disclosure to the spouse may be more dependent on the ambient attitudes toward homosexuality. As can be seen from Table 11.3, this does tend to

Table 11.2 **Number and proportion married or separated**

	Married	*Separated*
Sweden	1 (0.6%)	12 (6.8%)
Australia	3 (2.0%)	18 (11.5%)
Finland	7 (4.9%)	11 (7.8%)

χ^2_2 = 6.59, p<.05

Table 11.3 **Number responding to question: 'Did your wife know you were homosexual?'**

	Yes	*Uncertain/No*
Sweden	13	0
Australia	11	10
Finland	13	5

χ^2_2 = 8.88, p<.05

follow the expected pattern. In response to the question, 'Did your wife know you were homosexual?', there is a significant difference between groups, with almost half the Australians indicating that they were uncertain or that she did not know, compared with about one-third of the Finns and none of the Swedes. Thus it would appear that self-disclosure is also affected by the societal environment regarding homosexuality.

Surprisingly, the number of individuals who responded to the question, 'Have you ever been engaged?' in each country was not significantly different (see Table 11.4). It may be that the number who actually went through with the marriage, rather than those who were to some degree attracted to women sufficiently to consider a permanent liaison, is the significant indicator of societal pressure against homosexuality. At this stage it is probably important to note that there were no significant differences between the total samples in the three countries on the Kinsey Scale (means: Sweden 5.41, Australia 5.28, Finland 5.46), although as Ross (1979) has noted, admission of degree of homosexuality may itself be susceptible to societal pressures.

Table 11.4 Number responding to question: 'Have you ever been engaged?'

	Yes	*No*
Sweden	28 (17.4%)	146 (82.6%)
Australia	27 (18.4%)	129 (81.6%)
Finland	24 (17.1%)	118 (82.9%)

χ_2^2 = 0.09, n.s.

Thus far, it is apparent that in terms of the social and societal environment with regard to homosexuality, there is an affect on proportion of homosexuals marrying, with the greatest proportion in the most anti-homosexual society and the smallest proportion in the least anti-homosexual one, and that this trend is also apparent in terms of separations (which follow the reverse trend, with most in the most anti-homosexual society) and in terms of the spouse being told about her husband's homosexual preference. While the effects of sampling may have some contribution to make (although this cannot be known), it would appear reasonable to conclude that in the more anti-homosexual societies there will be a greater proportion of homosexuals marrying (and separating, probably as a function of more homosexuals in those societies marrying for reasons which were not sustainable through the marriage), and fewer will reveal their sexual preference to their wives. These data appear consistent with the findings of Weinberg and Williams (1974), which gives them somewhat more weight.

What, then, are the differences between the married and separated groups, between those who were involved with women by being married or engaged and those never involved, and between those who were engaged and those who were married? Do any differences found substantiate or validate the findings of the previous study? In terms of demographic and individual characteristics, those individuals who were still married had an average age of 38.0, became homosexually active on average at 25.3 and had realised they were predominantly homosexual at the average age of 15.4. In contrast, those who had been married but were now separated, using averages again, were aged 34.4, became homosexually active at 23.2 and realised they were predominantly homosexual at age 15.4: there was no statistically significant difference between the groups in this regard, nor on years of education, degree of religious commitment, or social class. In contrast, those who had never married were significantly younger on average (29.9), had become homosexually active at a somewhat younger age (19.8), and had also realised that they were predominantly homosexual somewhat younger, at age 13.5 on average. This does suggest, as in the previous data, that those who married tended to recognise or accept their homosexual feelings later, and to act on them later.

Looking first at the scales differentiating those who were either engaged or married compared with those who were never engaged or married, only two differences emerge. First, masculinity as measured by the Bem Sex Role Inventory (Bem, 1974, 1977) was significantly higher in those who had been engaged or married. This rather interesting finding suggests that marriage may be seen as a part of the conventional masculine image, and that becoming involved in this way with a woman is to some degree fulfilling a role or stereotype. Second, there is a significant difference on the factor measuring actual societal reaction experienced against homosexuality in those who were engaged or married, suggesting that perhaps marriage or engagement may have been a response to actual negative reactions by significant others. However, it is not possible to ascertain whether these responses may have been prior to engagement or marriage or subsequently. Nor can one be sure whether this result suggests that those who have had the more negative reactions from others to their homosexuality may not have got this reaction because they were married and homosexual, rather than just homosexual. Finally, given that there appeared to be no effect on the proportion of homosexual men having been engaged across the three cultures, it may be that it is not appropriate to look at the engaged group as different from those who never married and never became engaged. For this reason, it may be more appropriate to compare those who were engaged with those who were or had been married (the married and separated groups combined). This approach has the added advantage, given the relatively small numbers involved, of comparing groups of roughly equal size (70 engaged versus 52 ever married).

Comparing the engaged group with those who had been married, a number of significant differences were apparent. Probably of most importance is the fact that 'expected societal reaction' (ESR) differentiated the two groups significantly, with those who had married showing a higher ESR than those who had been engaged. A similar trend was also apparent on 'actual societal reaction' (ASR). The actual measurement of ASR and ESR followed the form described in the earlier study, with individuals ticking the position on the scale which described the way the individual listed *had* reacted if they knew the respondent was homosexual for ASR (divided by the number of ticks). For ESR, the same pattern followed, but using a cross for the way the respondent thought individuals listed *would* react: the method is described in detail by Ross (1983b), as is the derivation of the factor scales measuring aspects of societal reaction. The first two of these factors measure 'actual societal reaction' and ESR respectively.

It will be recalled that conservatism generally did not produce any significant differences at all in the previous analysis of married homosexual men. In the Scandinavian-Australian study reported in this chapter, a specific measure of conservatism, sex-role conservatism (MacDonald, 1974) was used. This scale, as well as a total sex-role conservatism, gives four sub-scales measuring sex-role conservatism with regard to equality in business and the professions, sex-appropriate behaviour, social and domestic work, and power in the home. Comparing those who were or had been married with those only engaged, three of these as well as the total sex-role conservatism score differentiate the two groups: equality in business and the professions, sex-appropriate behaviour, and power in the home. On each of these measures the married group were significantly higher in sex-role conservatism, which again tends to confirm that marriage may have been a response to seeing a narrower role for males than other homosexuals, such a narrow role including marriage

Table 11.5 **Scales differentiating engaged or married sample versus never engaged or married sample**

Masculinity	Involved	4.33	p<.05
	Never involved	4.09	
Factor 1	Involved	7.01	p<.05
(Actual societal reaction)	Never involved	6.73	

Table 11.6 **Scales differentiating still married versus separated samples**

Masculinity	Married	4.07	p<.075
	Separated	4.47	
Factor 3	Married	3.19	p<.05
(Depressed inadequacy)	Separated	4.27	
1 Conservatism	Married	17.45	p<.01
(Equality in business)	Separated	7.91	
2 Conservatism	Married	19.45	p<.01
(Sex-appropriate behaviour)	Separated	11.51	
3 Conservatism	Married	15.91	p<.01
(Social-domestic work)	Separated	8.35	
4 Conservatism	Married	22.82	p<.01
(Power in home)	Separated	9.33	
Total conservatism	Married	75.64	p<.01
	Separated	37.09	

as part of male role behaviour. It is of particular significance that previous research (MacDonald and Games, 1974) has noted that individuals who tend to be more sex-role conservative also tend to be more anti-homosexual. What is seen here would then also tend to suggest that sex-role conservatism and its attendent anti-homosexual attitudes may be one factor which contributes toward marriage of homosexual men and staying married.

This latter point is strongly reinforced when the factors which differentiate those who are still married from those who have separated are considered. Looking at these two groups (which have not been broken down by country due

Table 11.7 **Scales differentiating married and separated sample versus those only engaged**

Factor 1 (Actual societal reaction)	Ever married Engaged	7.21 6.76	p<.075
Factor 2 (Expected societal reaction)	Ever married Engaged	6.04 5.55	p<.05
1 Conservatism (Equality in business)	Ever married Engaged	11.09 9.00	p<.075
3 Conservatism (Social-domestic work)	Ever married Engaged	11.46 8.68	p<.05
4 Conservatism (Power in home)	Ever married Engaged	14.08 11.37	p<.075
Total conservatism	Ever married Engaged	51.00 41.67	p<.05

to the small numbers), all four sub-scales of sex-role conservatism as well as total sex-role conservatism score are differentiators, to the extent that in all of the scales the married group's scores are double those of the separated group. If this result was caused *by* marriage, rather than was a cause *of* it, it would be expected that those who had been married but were now separated would have had similarly elevated scores. Again, the masculinity score differentiates the two groups, but in this analysis, surprisingly, the separated group has the higher score. Interpretation of this is puzzling: perhaps it indicates that the separated group are more assertive than those who remain married, but this remains conjecture only. Similarly, the only factor which distinguishes the two groups is that measuring depressed inadequacy, with the separated group having the higher score. This would tend to suggest that psychological well-being is lower in those men who had separated, although this finding was not noted in the previous data, and the implications remain obscure. It may be that remaining married provides a degree of security which separation lacks.

In summary, not only can it be demonstrated that the anti-homosexual social and societal environments lead to higher proportions of homosexual men marrying (and separating), as well as less openness about their sexual orientation to their spouses, but also that the variables of societal reaction, both actual and expected, are again apparent as differentiators between groups and by implication as factors involved in the marriage of homosexual men. One factor which is particularly salient in the Scandinavian-Australian analysis is that of sex-role conservatism. While general conservatism was previously shown not to be implicated, sex-role conservatism is clearly an important predictor of marriage along with societal reaction. This is of particular interest since Ross, Rogers and McCulloch (1978) have indicated that they believe the two main factors which determine the role a homosexual projects in a society, or which a society projects on to the individual, are determined by the degree of anti-homosexual prejudice and the degree of sex-role conservatism in that society acting together. The finding reported in this chapter would also suggest, then, that those two factors may be implicated in the role the homosexual male plays in more general terms, such as in marriage and remaining married as well.

12 The effect of marriage on homosexuality: perspectives on therapy

So far, what has been considered has been the characteristics of married homosexual men: what differentiates those who stay married from those who separate, those who knew of their homosexuality before they married as opposed to after they married, and the differences that telling their wives at different stages of their relationship, or not at all have. The effects of varying degrees of homosexual preference have also been looked at. The final questions which must be answered at a more applied level are raised in this chapter. These include an examination of the effect of marriage on homosexuality, some general perspectives on therapy for homosexuals, and a more specific discussion of therapeutic approaches for married homosexual men.

Previous studies of homosexuality, particularly those prior to 1975, have emphasised as treatment of a same-sex erotic preference, techniques designed to remove homosexual arousal. Follow-up studies, which seldom followed up for more than eighteen months, generally indicated that the treatments were not particularly successful. At best, they could remove homosexual behaviour by aversive means but not replace it, and the only successes (somewhat narrowly defined as not having homosexual relationships) were with individuals who were at least bisexual. While there is little point in going into these studies in detail, the important point to note with regard to attempts to remove homosexual behaviour, whether or not heterosexual behaviour can be substituted, is its ethical implications.

These have been discussed in detail by Davison (1976) and

Ross (1977). Davison (1982) indicates that one cannot pretend that a therapist who tries to remove a patient's homosexuality is neutral in making such a decision. What such a therapist is doing is making a value judgment about the naturalness or otherwise of homosexuality. He notes that clinicians should pay more attention to the quality of human relationships than to the particular gender of the adult partners, and that most mental health professionals do not consider homosexuality an illness, simply a normal variant of human sexual behaviour. From this perspective, he suggests, one ends up having to deal with the tremendous legal and social oppression of homosexuals as a contributor to requests to change sexual orientation. In such an environment, therapeutic neutrality is a myth which cannot be sustained, since the therapist, if acceding to such a request, is acting as an agent of society. A therapist in such a situation is also simply reinforcing the view that homosexuality is deviant by agreeing to treat it.

To suggest that a person comes voluntarily to change his sexual orientation ignores the powerful societal pressures which devalue that orientation. Dissatisfaction with a homosexual orientation, which is often the presenting symptom, must be seen as a symptom and not homosexuality as the cause of the problems. This was demonstrated by Serber and Keith (1974), who observed that unhappiness with a homosexual orientation was usually related to an inability to express oneself adequately as a homosexual, or to loneliness or isolation from a homosexual subculture: attempts to treat the homosexuality rather than getting at the root of the dissatisfaction are treating symptom and not cause. Russell and Winkler (1977) also illustrated this by using both assertiveness training and non-directive coping groups for homosexuals who had trouble accepting their orientation, and reported that both groups showed an increase in happiness with homosexual functioning. Thus therapists should be wary of married homosexual men who believe that removal of their same-sex erotic preference (even if it were possible) will solve their problems. Meeting such a request would not only be treating a symptom rather than a basic problem, but also reinforcing the patient's negative beliefs about homosexuality which are one of the basic causes of dissatisfaction and heterosexual marriage of homosexual men. It is necessary, however, to look at the evidence of change of sexual preference in the married homosexual.

Many reviews of attempts to change individuals from homosexual have emphasised the provision of a positively reinforced modelling situation so that the subject can learn the necessary response patterns and behaviours to facilitate heterosexual interaction and provide for its continuation as a self-reinforcing chain. Denholtz (1973) for example, has advocated the extension of a variety of covert processes including guided imagery and orgasmic reconditioning to guide subjects from the stage of negative reaction to homosexuality to positive reaction to heterosexuality, although Marshall (1973) has noted that alteration of fantasies on their own does not necessarily have an effect on behaviour. The general implication of earlier studies that once heterosexual approach is commenced and heterosexual behaviour begins therapy may cease, is stated by Rehm and Rozensky (1974). In their study, multiple modification techniques were used (including reducing heterosexual anxiety, deconditioning homosexual approach, altering homosexual fantasies and modifying masturbatory fantasies) to provide the most comprehensive coverage of all conditions which could affect the homosexual to heterosexual shift. From this point on, they suggest, heterosexuality shoud have been self-reinforcing.

Thus, if conditions could be provided in which there were heterosexual attachment, heterosexual physical involvement and strong motivation to change orientation to heterosexual, then this would be the optimum situation for such permanent change to occur, if such a change was possible. This situation often occurs in the case of the heterosexually married homosexual man.

When the responses to the question, 'What was the effect of marriage on your homosexuality?' are tabulated (see Table 12.1), it is apparent that the suggestion that marriage should if anything decrease homosexual interest and arousal by increasing heterosexual interest and arousal is not confirmed by these data. In order to check whether the degree of homosexuality had any influence on the reported direction

121

Table 12.1 **Effect of marriage on homosexuality**

Direction	%
Increase	25
Decrease	5
No change	70

of change, a chi-squared test was performed on position on the Kinsey Scale by the direction of change (more homosexual, less homosexual, or no change): there was not a statistically significant result, indicating that direction of change does not depend on how homosexual the individual reports himself to be. In fact, contrary to the suggestions in the literature, homosexuality was actually *increased* by marriage in one quarter of the cases. How can this finding be explained?

In order to be satisfied by retention of null hypotheses one must be able to show that there are no areas of bias which could account for these results. In this research, there are two areas that could be noted in this regard. First, the sample might well have been biased towards those respondents who remained homosexual; those in whom there was a change of orientation would not have had the same chance of being included in the sample, because they would have minimal contact with the homosexual subculture. Nevertheless, by using acquaintance networks, a large number of previously homosexual men should have had a chance of inclusion. On questioning all respondents, none was aware of any person in whom marriage had led to a successful change of orientation.

Second, it could be argued that there had been no removal of the homosexual component in the sample by behavioural or therapeutic means. However, it has been demonstrated in the literature (Marshall, 1973) that all that can be expected in behaviour modification is a suppression of homosexual behaviour and re-emphasis on the heterosexual side. Given the strong desire for change implied in those homosexuals who have been shown to bow to social pressure in an attempt to meet the accepted and reinforced model (Ross, 1978), it would seem fair to assume that the negative social sanctions and the respondents' acceptance of these in marrying as well as the positive social reinforcement on marriage, would be at least as strong as any technique in a clinical setting.

Thus the suggestions from the research were not confirmed. The great majority of the respondents (70 per cent) felt that marriage had not altered their degree of homosexuality, and in fact a quarter felt that it had increased it (see Table 12.1). Only 5 per cent felt that marriage had had any effect in the hypothesised direction on their orientation. One cannot, therefore, conclude that marriage has any effect on homosexuality despite the ideal reinforcement situation. In fact, one could perhaps go further and take this to indicate that homosexuality is in most cases unmodifiable by even the most ideal social paradigm. That level on the Kinsey Scale was not a significant contributing factor (and was therefore controlled for) was shown by the lack of a significant difference in the direction of change of homosexuality by Kinsey Scale position.

As regards the reasons for the finding that in one quarter of the married respondents, their homosexuality increased during marriage, some responses are given in Table 12.2: it would appear to be the case that at some point in every marriage the husband's homosexuality became more important to him. Significantly, the two reasons most commonly given relate to the difficulty of keeping homosexual feelings in the background, regardless of the positively reinforcing aspects of marriage. Marriage strains, indicating that the marriage is developing more negative than positive reinforcing attributes, were listed as important by less than 18 per cent of the sample; and a breakdown of this revealed that the figure is accounted for by those respondents who had separated from their wives. The last ranked two reasons were listed equally by married and separated samples and again refer to negative aspects of marriage. Thus, while less than 40 per cent of the respondents listed reasons for increase in the importance of their homosexuality which related to negatively reinforcing aspects of marriage, the majority noted factors which related to positively reinforcing aspects of homosexuality. This supports the suggestion that, regardless of the positive aspects of marriage as an

Table 12.2 **Reasons for increase in importance of homosexuality during marriage**

Statement	%
Couldn't keep homosexual feelings at bay	41.0
Meeting a particular gay person	20.5
Marriage strains	17.6
Wife's frigidity	13.8
Marriage began to grow stale	7.1

exceptional form of orientation-change therapy, there is a strong tendency not to respond to modification attempts. One might, of course, argue that greater social acceptance of homosexuality led to its becoming more important during marriage. However, 32 per cent of those who had separated said they had thought of remarriage, which tends to suggest that this is not a valid argument.

If we accept these results as an accurate indication of the problem, then the implications for modification of homosexual behaviour or orientation are considerable, suggesting that no modification of sex orientation is possible, except perhaps in the short term (follow-ups from previous studies have seldom lasted for more than eighteen months). Researchers in the area of behaviour modification have already turned their attention from total change to a more realistic role in adapting homosexuals to their orientation rather than away from it (Serber and Keith, 1974). The non-rejection of the second part of the hypothesis does show that the findings were not due, as in Imieliński's (1969) data, to level of homosexuality. Nevertheless, his work does indicate that the greater the homosexuality-based strains in a marriage and the smaller the heterosexual basis, the more likely a breakup will occur.

In many cases, therefore, despite the presence of a paradigm from which one would expect positive results, there is not a modification but something more akin to a multiplication of homosexuality, despite the fact that getting rid of homosexuality was often the most important reason for and pressure towards marriage. In the marriage, increase in the importance of homosexuality was usually against the wishes of the husband and a function of the presence of a homosexual orientation rather than of marriage strains. This tends to lend weight to the suggestions that homosexuality may be unmodifiable, and that marriage, in order to de-emphasise a homosexual orientation, is ineffective.

Perhaps the best way to explain these results from a theoretical point of view is to adopt the approach of Shively and DeCecco (1977). They suggested that homosexuality and heterosexuality should not be seen conceptually as the two extremes of a single continuum, with the amount of homosexuality the inverse of the amount of heterosexuality, but as two separate dimensions. Thus the amount of homosexual preference is independent of the amount of heterosexual preference: one can go up or down without necessarily affecting the other. While in Western society people are socialised into believing that an individual is either homosexual *or* heterosexual, there is no reason why one orientation should be dependent on the other. This would also help to explain why previous attempts to change homosexuals to heterosexuals by trying to remove the homosexual component of a person's life-style in the assumption that this will automatically increase any heterosexual component, have not been successful. Of course, if there is no heterosexual component, it will be very difficult to create one, too.

Given that behavioural approaches to altering an individual's sexual preference are both unsuccessful and probably also unethical, what approaches have been used for treating married homosexual men who have problems with being both married and homosexual? In this regard it must be borne in mind that being married and homosexual by no means necessarily creates problems, and that many married homosexual men by compartmentalising their lives or by having an open or understanding relationship with their wives manage as well or better than many conventionally married heterosexual couples. Excluding those who do not have problems in being married and homosexual, what are the appropriate approaches?

Richardson and Hart (1981) discuss generally the problems of married and isolated homosexuals, seeing the two categories as being essentially similar since both isolated and

125

married homosexuals have similar experiences: living a life-style which is not congruent with an individual's identification as homosexual. They also indicate that, in their experience, marriage for individuals who have difficulty in accepting their same-sex interests usually leads to a compounding of the problem. The evidence from the present study tends to support this to some degree.

Other problems which they discuss are also particularly pertinent. For example, the images of homosexuals which are likely to be available may be stereotypic, such as the overly effeminate male, and the individual may not be able to identify with such an image. Or there may be psychological strains involved in not revealing parts of one's self-identity. Conversely, there may also be strains involved in revealing it, although the data reported in the present study do not offer overwhelming support that this is common to any more than a small proportion of married homosexual men. The sample reported here, however, is a sample from the community, and it may not be wise to generalise from them to the problems faced by homosexual men who do seek help, whether through their medical practitioner, minister of religion, welfare officer or telephone counselling service. Initially, the presentation may be to be 'cured' of their homosexuality, but as has been observed earlier on in this chapter, this tends to be treating the perceived symptom and not the cause of the problem.

Generally, Richardson and Hart advocate that account should be taken of the costs and benefits of being secretive or open for the particular individual, although in Chapter 10 it was made clear that there is likely to be a great difference between perceived and actual costs and benefits: this will be discussed in greater detail presently. The crux of the matter, they suggest, is likely to be the conflict married homosexuals feel in the commitment they feel able to make to a homosexual life-style, in addition to being involved in a heterosexual married life-style. Decisions may in some cases also be made whether to seek outside of the marriage same-sex relationships. Once the decision to reveal a homosexual preference to the spouse has been made, if it is to be made, it may also be necessary to cope with rejection, disbelief, and the risk of separation and perhaps loss of children. As Richardson and Hart point out, these reactions will to some degree depend on the current state of the couple's sexual and emotional relationship. Problems may also arise in connection with the homosexual world, for example, a married man may be seen by possible partners as posing problems such as a divided commitment between the potential partner and wife and family. Choices, of course, will have to be made. Some of these will include, according to Richardson and Hart (1981):

> wishing to continue the married relationship whilst identifying as homosexual but choosing not to indulge in same-sex acts, having an 'open' marriage which does include the possibility of such relationships, or dissolving the marriage. Alternatively, s/he may choose to remain married and seek treatment for homosexual feelings (p. 169).

One of the few studies to date to actually look at the process of therapy and its outcome in married homosexual and bisexual men is that of Coleman (1982). While this is based on a therapy sample, it would appear from Coleman's data that in many ways the married homosexual men in his group are comparable to the group reported in the present study. For this reason, it is probably appropriate to describe his group in some detail. Of the thirty-one individuals in Coleman's study, all were to some degree aware of same-sex erotic feelings, and all but four had acted on these feelings, before they were married. He points out that the *meaning* of this activity, however, was different to them and they did not take it to imply that they were homosexuals. All married in response to societal and family pressures and the perceived lack of intimacy in the homosexual world, and all reported that they had married their wives because they loved them. Interest in having and raising children was also mentioned by several. The thought that marriage would help overcome their homosexual feelings played a part in several men's marriages: it is of interest that again in Coleman's study the influence of societal pressure against homosexuality plays a very significant part in the decision to marry.

Attempts to eliminate homosexual feelings, he reports,

had been present to the extent where over one-third of his sample had actually tried to eliminate their same-sex erotic feelings through various forms of psychotherapy, and none had been successful. It could be postulated that those men who had attempted to remove their homosexual preference would be the ones who were most likely to enter therapy: the mechanism for this may even have been the reinforcement of their guilt about their homosexual preference by therapists attempting to remove their homosexual feelings.

Other aspects of Coleman's sample which suggest that it is comparable to that in the present study include the fact that average age was 38.6, average length of marriage 13.1 years, and average number of children two. Only 16 per cent of the wives knew of their husband's homosexuality prior to marriage. The vast majority (94 per cent) had extra-marital liaisons, and nearly two-thirds had sexual conflicts within the marriage (particularly erectile dysfunction) which may have been a factor contributing to their seeking treatment.

Treatment took the form of a ten-week 'bisexuality group', and issues, according to Coleman, included increased comfort with their homosexuality, exploration of ways of incorporating homosexual and heterosexual feelings into patients lives, examination of some of the myths of sexual preference, and gaining better understanding of human sexual functioning, and particularly sexual performance, in both homo- and heterosexual relationships. The methods chosen to accomplish these goals included education, sharing of experiences and concerns, and assertiveness training: follow-up of this group varied from a period of several months to 2½ years post-treatment.

Following treatment, Coleman reports, 36 per cent decided to end their marriages (although half had been seriously considering this on entering treatment). Three of the remainder who continued in marriage, however, felt this to be a temporary state of affairs, and only five of this remaining group intended having a monogamous relationship with their wives: several intended to act on their homosexual feelings without their wives' knowledge. Sixteen of the twenty-four men with children decided to stay married.

On follow-up of the men who remained committed to

their marriages, 30 per cent were divorced or in process of separating, and only two still committed to a monogamous relationship with their wives. Six were pursuing homosexual relationships, including close emotional ones which were causing marital difficulties; three had 'open-marriage' contracts with their wives, which may have been a preliminary to separation. Measures of sexual behaviour revealed no change in erotic fantasies (in all cases more homosexual than heterosexual), but a significant change towards more homosexual behaviour: emotional attachment appeared to be somewhat more homosexual.

Coleman suggests that the important factors involved in successful adjustment to remaining married include both partners loving each other, communicating, wanting to make the relationship work, and having resolved feelings of guilt and resentment. The wife must have a sense of worth outside of marriage, and voluntary physical contact between the partners is also necessary. If outside sexual contacts occur, the wife will either not know about them, or have developed an open-marriage contract. Probably most important, both partners must be prepared to work on and to accept the husband's same-sex feelings.

While Coleman's study and approach to therapy is invaluable in indicating both the similarities between the characteristics of his clients to those of the respondents in the present study (although his clients show a greater level of concern than those reported here, the basis of the concerns are similar) and in delineating possible outcomes, it is necessary to go beyond this. What has been discovered in the research reported in this book has important implications for therapy with married homosexual men. The implications of these findings are outlined below.

Perhaps the most important finding in terms of therapy is that there is, in general, not a great degree of psychopathology as a result of marriage: in fact there appears to be no essential difference between those who are still married, separated, and have never married. The strains of leading a potentially conflicting existence appear to be well taken care of by compartmentalisation, and except in situations of stress, such as when a spouse is made aware of her husband's sexual preferences and reacts negatively, psycho-pathology is unlikely to be present. However, of equal importance is the variable of societal reaction. Throughout the various analyses, it has been apparent that the strongest predictor of what leads to marriage (and inversely, to later separation) is an expectation that significant others will react negatively to the individual's homosexuality. This, rather than the way people have actually reacted, will need to be desensitised before the individual can begin to accept his homosexual erotic preferences. The mechanism of expected negative societal reaction also needs to be understood before therapy can be effective. In many cases, there will be two stems to expected negative societal reaction against homo-sexuality, an internal and an external one. The internal stem may be based on the individual's lack of acceptance of homo-sexuality as normal or valid as a life-style, which is projected on to other individuals or society in general. As Richardson and Hart (1981) have already pointed out, there may be two specific contributors: an inability to accept homosexuality because of the belief that homosexuals lead lonely lives, and an inability to recognise oneself as homosexual because the mythical stereotype of the homosexual male as a flam-boyant and effeminate hairdresser simply does not apply. Both these contributors are themselves a function of the prevailing degree of anti-homosexual feeling in a society, and thus the second (external) stem is the perceived societal reaction to homosexuality. This will to a large degree be determined by the family, religious, socio-economic and educational background of the individual, but the laws of the state and official and media reaction to homosexuality will also have an important effect. Of course, it is not possible to separate out internal and external stems, as they intertwine at many levels. Nevertheless, perhaps the most critical aspect of therapy will include obtaining the indivi-dual's views of what is negative and positive about homo-sexuality (and heterosexuality) and building upon or altering his cognitive schemata of human sexualities. This is best achieved by education and by experience with others in the same situation. If it has not already happened, exposure to normal homosexuals is often an important step in self-acceptance. It may be, of course, that over a period of a number of years of marriage the individual has reached the point of accepting that his primary sexual preference is homosexual, in which case the therapeutic relationship may then focus on crisis management if a crisis within the relationship has developed, or discussion of alternatives if a point of decision has been reached.

To a large degree, where decisions on continuation of marriage or separation have been reached, the patient is the *relationship* rather than the *individual*, and wherever possible the couple should be seen rather than the individual. One danger is that the patient's homosexuality may be seen as the primary cause of marital disharmony whereas it may in fact be the factor or scapegoat chosen to explain or express a number of other marital problems which are not necessarily related. It is always important to ascertain whether homosexuality is the central reason for the presentation of problems or just a cloak which takes the blame for all sorts of difficulties of personality or incompatibility. However, once it has been established that homosexuality of one partner is the central presenting problem, it is often necessary to make it clear that homosexuality need not preclude heterosexuality, and that there are points of compromise along a continuum from remaining married in a monogamous relationship to complete separation. As it often takes some months or longer for spouses to come to terms with a husband's homosexuality, the level of compromise may alter significantly over months or years. In fact, Coleman's (1982) data suggest that adjustment within the marriage becomes a process of moving along such a continuum until the point of mutual agreement is reached. Clearly, the single greatest determinant of this will be the spouse and her attitudes. She will usually face strong feelings of rejection and lack of worth, and these will need to be both recognised and attended to. Therapy with the husband may often be fruitless unless his spouse is receiving support from another professional or from the therapist if he or she is able to offer conjoint therapy. Decisions based upon guilt, blame or resentment usually seldom last, and can often be avoided if the spouse's needs are attended to simultaneously.

If there is still some degree of love and physical contact between the partners, then compromises may be reached. In the absence of this, however, it is unlikely that meaningful compromises within marriage can occur. If separation does occur, then the usual stages of loss and grief must be expected. To a large extent this will depend on the strength of the relationship and whether there is a co-existing homosexual relationship. In some cases, however, the isolation after a marriage breaks up will lead to loneliness, depression and self-recrimination, and one of the most important factors to ensure good outcome is to be prepared to provide active support after separation. This may involve the use of groups for others in the same situation, and the active use of homosexual social support agencies where available. Unfortunately, the commercial homosexual social scene in most cities caters to the under-thirties, and it is not unlikely that homosexual men who have married and separated will be above this age. Therapy for married homosexual men will be as individual as the people involved, and it is impossible to give more than a general outline here. However, it is likely to take place over a long period of time, and involve education in the initial stages and support in the latter stages. It may also involve conjoint therapy with the spouse.

One of the problems in dealing with marriages of homosexual men is the presence of children. While it is not the purpose of this book to examine this point in great detail, a number of questions are often asked. Usually the first question is whether having an openly homosexual parent (or parents) is likely to disturb the children or to lead to their being homosexual themselves. There is some experimental literature bearing on this point, most notably the work of Green (1978). Green looked at some thirty-eight children where one or both parents were homosexual or even transsexual (living as a member of the opposite sex): he found that there were no disturbances of either sex role (masculinity or femininity) or of sexual preference in any of the children, after some time of follow-up. It would appear that having one or both parents who are homosexual has no effect on the children. Current research theorising would suggest that the important variable in normal child development is the quality of the relationship between parents and children rather than the sex roles displayed or the number or sex of the parents or who they relate to sexually and emotionally.

There have also been a number of well-designed studies carried out by Miller (1978, 1979a, b) which look in some detail at the problems and adaptations of homosexual fathers. Miller found that the fifty homosexual fathers he interviewed ranged in age from 24 to 64, and that there was an enormous range of overtness and various living and child custody arrangements, as well as a similar range of problems faced in these arrangements. It is probably not possible to make general comments about homosexual fathers given such a range of adaptations.

In summary, then, it can be demonstrated that it is neither particularly responsible ethically nor possible experimentally to remove homosexual orientation. Heterosexual orientation may, within certain limits, be enhanced in some cases, but this is probably the exception rather than the rule. Marriage does not modify homosexual preference from the evidence presented here, and it is preferable to approach the married homosexual man in therapy through seeking to modify his cognitive schema of homosexuality and heterosexuality. From this, the marriage can be approached from a position of compromise where this is possible. Emphasis on education and support in the long term are necessary, rather than attempts to alter or suppress the patient's sexual orientation, which will only reinforce the view that his orientation is unacceptable and lead to a descending spiral of guilt and increased stress. While each case of therapy will be different, attention to modifying expected anti-homosexual societal reaction and providing support when necessary are usually key elements in a successful outcome.

13 Interviews with married homosexuals — some case studies

From the discussion of the clinical and theoretical aspects of the adaptations and adjustments of the married homosexual male it may appear that the majority of such respondents lead unhappy or double lives. Any such implications could only be gained from regarding group trends as indicative of the state of all members of the group: clearly, such an assumption would be totally unwarranted. In interviewing respondents it was clear that, while many did have some problems arising from conflicts between their homosexuality and marriage, many did not. Some respondents found that being both married and homosexual was an advantage in terms of getting the most out of life, and showed this in their stability, maturity and lack of any adjustment problems at all. Since, in such a series of data analyses as have been carried out, respondents tend to be seen as neatly stereotyped and typical clinical entities, several case histories that are representative of the phenomenon of the person with homosexual tendencies who marries heterosexually, have been included. In including them, it is hoped that the emphasis of the problems of the married homosexual will not overshadow the total personality or the stability of other married homosexuals who do not see their situation either as a disadvantage or a problem.

Case History One

K is a 53-year-old university graduate who has been happily married for thirty years. His wife, also a university graduate is, like her husband, involved in full-time professional work. They have three children, all of whom are married and living away from home, although in the same city as their parents. Both K and his wife are active in community affairs, and have a wide circle of friends.

When K married at the age of 23 he was aware of some attraction to other males, and had had a couple of brief homosexual encounters at university and during active service in the Armed Forces. While one of these incidents was mentioned to his future wife at the time of their engagement, she indicated that she was not prepared to accept K's homosexual inclinations and has not raised the subject with reference to K since, although she is tolerant of homosexuality in others.

To describe K as a 'married homosexual' would be misleading. He is more properly a person who has the ability to relate to people of either sex, and who, in a predominantly heterosexual existence, has had some homosexual relationships, only one of which occurred after marriage. There seems to be no great difficulty in coping with both homosexual and heterosexual elements in K's life, as there is with some people: instead, the two seem to complement each other. Nor does this lead to problems in expressing himself or developing meaningful relationships. Rather the opposite is true: later, it will become obvious that K's homosexual relationship has revitalised his marriage at a time when many other marriages may have become staid, and rejuvenated his work, rather than affected them in any detrimental way.

Unfortunately, at best a case history can provide material facts, but must be written according to the formulae of the publication manuals and accepted convention. Since the individuals described often become grey and characterless as a function of the style required, if nothing worse, it seems best for the individual to describe himself and his experiences in his own words and as he sees them.

Below are extracts from K's letters to V, a 23-year-old graduate with whom K had a deep and close relationship. Better than anything else, they describe K's situation and his reactions to the relationship, demonstrating that marriage and homosexuality do not necessarily cause problems, but may lead to fulfilment of all aspects of a person's needs. Here, in fact, homosexuality might be seen as an operation of multiplication, rather than division, of human potential and growth:

> there was what I can describe only as a flash of contact, an instant vibration; somehow, like had met like. You pranced around me for the rest of that afternoon with a sparkle and animation that was irresistible, but when, in leaving, I asked that you ring me, who had started what? And, as I think I pointed out to you in that superlative dialogue, all the swelling and extension of the friendship came from you . . . .

> Now I should like to sweep out of the way a few hypocrisies — not yours, mine. If, as Christine Taylor says, one must find the qualities in oneself that one loves in the other, it follows that what one dislikes in the other, are qualities in oneself also, and to express them, as belonging to the other, is a feint of the self to protect and justify it. Example: I have often thought, and even said once to your face, that you are a little whore. Pot calling kettle black. Would I refuse were there to be another episode like yours? If someone like you came to my door? Not likely. I'd be in, balls and all, as they say.

> I couldn't be sure I wouldn't meet young people known, if not to me, then to my children, and for M's sake [K's wife], I couldn't expose her to the kind of compassionate curiosity of 'We know something about him that you don't know!'
> I'm also afraid that at times, I envy your freedom of movement. I seem to be stuck like the king on a chessboard, able to move only one square in any direction, where you can be the roving queen. (In a chess sense; no other.)

> I can recommend insecurity only because I have never taken that course myself. Always I have returned home, to safe haven, and I think I made it clear to you from the first that the one thing I would never do for you would be to jeopardise my marriage.

136

I am, it seems to me, the Hanged Man, upside down but radiant, unable to move, yet capable of warmth and light. [Referring to a Tarot card.]

A friendship as explicitly physical as ours became, can only flourish if it can take place in freedom, and I had behind me, or dragged with me, the ball and chain of wife and family. Thus you were right to bring up M's name in . . ., and while at the time I deeply resented what seemed to me moralising, a bit late after twelve weeks, this had always been there.

the whole framework of my life has changed with no kids to be responsible for . . . I would adore to have a super friendship with someone, but I can't go cruising around saunas, and anyway, this sort of thing is ignoble and, to say the least, lacks taste.

You remember I told you that I had completely dried up, and attempted to unload it, not on you personally, but on the totally unseizable and unsatisfactory nature of our relationship. Well, within two weeks I had written my best work for years, a rework of a draft I discarded some years ago, but a completely ripe and new work.

I can thank you for never using the obvious weapons to your hand. Although you have said and done many hurtful things, you have never made me feel either that my love for you was *wrong* or *ridiculous*. So, thanks.

Case History Two

P is a 27-year-old university graduate, separated from his wife. Like her husband, she is also a graduate involved in government. There are no children of the marriage, which took place when P was 22 and lasted four years.

P appears initially as a quiet, introverted and retiring person, but seems to have no difficulties in establishing social relationships with either heterosexuals or homosexuals. Before marriage, P was aware of interest in other males, but the full realisation that he was to some extent homosexual did not dawn until after marriage.

137

Marriage, to P and his wife, was not so much a result of pressure of any sort, but part of an orderly progression. They had known one another for four years, had gone out together, and had felt their lives bound up. In this situation, marriage was the next logical step. The relationship had not, however, included sex before the marriage. Because P was not at all experienced homosexually at the time, he felt that not only could he cope with marriage, but that he was more hetero- than homosexual. That a few homosexual contacts might occur on the side seemed inevitable, although they would not necessarily be of the 'one-night stand' variety. However, P did not realise that the sexual side of marriage would be such a strain as it was. Eventually, when he got used to the idea that sex and love were not the same thing, P sought and found homosexual relationships, since this was his only satisfactory sexual outlet. There was no guilt, as such, involved; it was just a matter of getting used to such affairs after the pressure to be faithful had weakened. In part, the conflict was due to P's strong religious involvement, but it was resolved internally: he saw himself, rather than the church, as right.

P does not see the conflict primarily as being both married and homosexual, but as being due also to 'growing up' processes. While he describes his own marriage as being 'hellish', P sees that some marriages can be good things: however, the idealised view of holy matrimony is felt by him to be an absurdity.

A year ago, after telling his wife he was homosexual and after some discussion and a period apart on holiday, P separated from her. He felt considerable relief when he told his wife, but not total relief until he was out of his marriage completely.

P sees the post-marital state as equally important as his experience of marriage. He feels closer to his wife than ever before, although this took six months of separation and a good deal of strain on both their parts. Two of the most important aspects of post-marital life are described below by P in a letter to the researcher.

As far as one's post-marital relations with others go, there is some considerable hesitancy about being too committed to another person on my part — even though I have been, most of the time. The effect of having been married seems to brood over one for a long time — maybe for years — which I didn't really expect.

At present, P is having a relationship with another male of his own age-group which has already lasted over a year. Generally, he does not divide the world into homosexual and heterosexual, as many others have, which may have helped reduce role-conflict: he sees himself as being the same person throughout, although now much happier and relaxed. While P valued, and will value more as he gets older, the companionship he found in marriage, he is now able to combine his emotional and sexual outlets in the one person. From his own report, he is now leading a fulfilling life.

Case History Three

H presented at an out-patient clinic terrified that he would be recognised by somebody and that people would immediately assume he was homosexual: he had been stimulated to present by hearing me discuss social pressure and homosexuality on a talk-back show a couple of weeks previously. H's problem concerned the fact that he was both homosexual and married, and that he wanted to have sexual relations with his wife again — they had had no intercourse for some two years. The problem was described by him as 'wanting to go back to being bisexual'.

Aged 55, H had been married for some twenty-five years. He had attended college, and been a successful executive in his profession. This had included living overseas for some years, until he had been able to retire to the country and to breed stud cattle in his mid-forties. Subsequent interests included politics, in which he was a prominent member of the executive of one of the more conservative parties.

H's homosexual experience commenced when he was a child, when at the age of about 10 he was involved in mutual sexual exploration with a garden helper who was slightly older — this occurred several times with mutual enjoyment. Nothing further occurred until the age of about 20, when he

139

had an encounter in a public toilet — from then on, he looked for such encounters, which might occur several times a month. He did not accept the fact that he was homosexual, and consulted a psychiatrist who told him it was not an illness, and to go and enjoy himself.

Marriage occurred at the age of 30 to a woman he worked with. Heterosexual relations had taken place on two occasions prior to marriage, and he had found them enjoyable. For four or five years following the marriage, which produced two daughters, H managed to suppress his homosexual activities, which he had thought were now under control. Gradually, the frequency of marital intercourse declined, and he found himself masturbating more frequently with attendant homosexual fantasies. By the age of 40 he was cruising public toilets on his way home from work, and marital intercourse had declined from about six times a year in the first years of marriage to only once or twice a year — he found himself developing headaches and going to bed early in order to avoid it. However, he also suppressed his homosexuality, and reports he still does to a degree. The only sexual expression was occasional guilt-ridden encounters in public toilets from time to time, usually a couple of times a month. From about the age of 40 these developed from mutual masturbation to oral and occasionally anal sex.

The move to the country coincided with a degree of acceptance of his homosexuality, which he had previously never discussed with anybody — in fact, his sense of relief on talking about it was obvious. At about 45, he met more regularly with two men in much the same situation who he had encountered during his public toilet encounters — they met in one another's offices for rapid sex whenever possible, which was not more than once every few months.

H described his views of heterosexual sex as being not really clean or part of marriage — in contrast, he was beginning to come to terms with homosexual relations. H's great problem was that he was unable to achieve erection now or to have intercourse with his wife — she had, according to him, accepted this philosophically. There had never been much experimentation in any case, with minimal foreplay and only missionary-position intercourse.

In terms of the future. H was adamant that he would in no way let anybody become aware of his homosexuality, in which he assessed himself as much more homosexual than heterosexual. However, he felt easier for having talked about what to him had been a secret he believed he would carry to the grave, but still felt that marriage was the only possible state for a man to be in, and that it was his primary responsibility in life.

Case History Four

A preferred to describe himself as bisexual, since he was both married and homosexual. He had been introduced to homosexuality at school while an adolescent, and since then had relationships with other males who were usually also close friends. At the age of 26 he married, and he and his wife emigrated when he was 28. Born into a lower middle-class family, A left school to work with his father at the age of 15, and has been continuously employed since then as a shopkeeper. There are three children of the marriage, two girls and a boy.

While A had sex with other boys at school and up to about the age of 19, he thought that this was a phase he was going through. He had also had sex with a female as a young adolescent, and enjoyed the experience. From his first homosexual relationship when he was 19, he continued to have sex with several close male friends but also had girlfriends as well — up to the age of 26, when he married, his sexual and emotional relationships were half homosexual and half heterosexual. Marriage lead to a cessation of homosexual relations for eighteen months, but after this he had a desire for homosexual sex much more intense than he had previously experienced. This led to his seeking contacts by cruising in parks and in public toilets: his wife was not aware of this. While the encounters were usually anonymous and casual ones, he also took up with some of his homosexual partners as friends. During this time, A was also having regular sex with his wife.

Four years ago, A told his wife that he was homosexual: she was horrified, but had suspected for some time. She came to terms with his sexual preference after about six weeks when she realised that it did not mean that his love for her had lessened, nor that he no longer wanted sex with her. Their marital sexual relations continued several times a week as previously, although now she would accept occasional homosexual affairs. She herself had indulged in a few extra-marital affairs which A had been aware of, which helped them to reconcile themselves to occasional infidelities. Shortly after this, however, there were two separations for a few weeks each when A's wife had an affair, but they reconciled because they found that they missed each other, and for the sake of the children who at that stage were aged between 5 and 11. Now, at the age of 40, A feels that he is more homosexual than heterosexual, although he still enjoys heterosexual relations. Emotionally, however, he describes himself as being equally attracted to both males and females. He has about six close friends of his own age or older whom he visits for homosexual encounters, and also occasionally cruises for homosexual outlets. The eldest daughter, aged 14, knows that her father is to a degree homosexual and appears to have no trouble in accepting this.

While the marriage is based on a mutual emotional and sexual bond, A feels that he is more interested in his homo-sexual acquaintances, and that if he was to have to make a decision to marry again, he would not do it and move toward becoming more homosexually involved. However, he and his wife and family have grown close over the fifteen years of marriage and he is happy with the mutual arrangement which allows both himself and his wife their sexual freedom.

Case History Five

B presented as an in-patient with severe anxiety and episodes of breaking down uncontrollably at work. His initial history indicated that he had been married for eighteen months to a co-worker (he was aged 35), and prior to that had lived with a male companion some years his senior, who had died tragically some two years before.

After gaining B's confidence, it transpired that he had been aware of attraction to other men since early adolescence,

142

and felt enormously guilty: his guilt was to some degree related to his strong religious beliefs. This lead him to a course of aversive behaviour modification to 'remove' his homosexuality at age 20, which did not affect his homosexual preference but made him feel much more guilty about it, to the extent where any brief encounters led to weeks of mental recrimination.

In the course of his work, B met D, an older man who to some degree represented the father B had never had, his own father having left shortly after he was born. They lived together in a happy and monogamous relationship for fourteen years, during which B completed college and entered the work-force as a junior executive. Tragically, however, D developed cancer and died. B was inconsolable, and suffered a depth of depression previously unknown to him. Some six months later, he married F, a woman of about his own age with whom he worked. There were difficulties almost from the start, with B only being able to obtain an erection by fantasising about males, and F trying to control the relationship as much as possible. She had previously had a boyfriend who was still married, and in the course of the eighteen months of her marriage with B left B four or five times to return to her boyfriend, eventually becoming pregnant (probably to the boyfriend, as B had difficulty reaching orgasm with her).

At this stage B was admitted to hospital, and F was insisting that the child was B's and that he should support her and the child. He resolved not to live with her, and made considerable progress once he had admitted his homosexuality and the nature of his past relationship — he and D had no contact with the homosexual subculture, and there were no friends who knew the real nature of his relationship with D. There was a period of several months where B was in therapy, and as a result of this he accepted that he was homosexual and began to take the first steps toward ameliorating the loneliness that he had found himself unable to cope with and which had led to his marriage. The process was assisted by contact with a sympathetic priest who also helped B to see his homosexuality in the wider context of human relationships rather than as a sexual sin. Gradually, through

143

introductions to various individuals B developed a small circle of friends who were also homosexual (the first contact he had had with a homosexual subculture) although he would not go to bars or homosexual meeting places.

Eventually, F bore a child which was shown on blood test not to be B's, and he has not seen her for some time — divorce proceedings are in hand. B hopes that in time he will meet somebody older than himself with whom he can settle down and live with in a relationship similar to that with D. At present, he is having problems accepting the transitory nature of many of the relationships he is having with other homosexuals, and particularly with loneliness. With therapeutic support, however, B is accepting his present situation and looking toward a long-term relationship with another male partner.

14 Conclusions

There have been many speculations in the literature with regard to the married homosexual man, few of which have been previously investigated. The primary purpose of this book has been the investigation of the adaptation and adjustment of the married homosexual in an attempt to answer many of these questions. From this, it should be possible to provide a guide to aid those professionals who may work with such individuals, and to cast more light on the effect of societal pressure on the individual. Many of the hypotheses proposed in earlier chapters have been subject to empirical test, and what follows is a brief synopsis of some of the central findings.

In considering those sub-groups of respondents who had found out about their homosexuality after marriage, those who had told their wives at various points in the relationship (or never), and those who considered themselves bisexual rather than homosexual, there were not a great number of differentiating features. This did suggest that such variations did not produce a great number of stresses, and that there is more homogeneity among such groups than expected.

The result has been to illuminate a previously little-understood phenomenon, and at the same time illustrate some of the ways societal pressures may be translated into life-styles. It may be that the problems it was felt married homosexuals faced are not as general as hypothesised — nevertheless, many of the findings of this study may, in terms of antecedents rather than consequences, have some utility for the understanding of unmarried homosexual men who have difficulty accepting their orientation. That, however, must remain a subject for further study.

A number of general points have been illustrated by the present study. First, it is clear that the married homosexual male in Australia and New Zealand is little different from his counterparts in other Western societies. The surprising degree of consistency between the data of earlier studies and the present study can only be interpreted as confirming the existence of common elements and reactions in male homosexuals in Western society.

Second, one of the major factors underlying the marriages of homosexuals has been demonstrated to be a highly anti-homosexual expected peer and societal reaction. It has been suggested that selective perception or some other background and environmental factors may have led to the 'personality type' of the marrying homosexual male being distinguishable in this regard from that of his unmarried counterparts. While expected negative societal reaction clearly differentiates between those homosexual men who are high and low in their resistance to social pressure, conformity to social norms in homosexuality appears to be highly situation-specific: there is no evidence that such conformity is a general characteristic of the married homosexual respondent in other areas. In general there is no evidence to connect this situation-specific conformity with conservatism. Rather the opposite; the samples seemed less conservative than their heterosexual contemporaries. The one exception, however, was sex-role conservatism, which was higher in married homosexuals than unmarried controls. Cross-cultural comparisons also tend to demonstrate that the degree of anti-homosexual feeling in a society has an effect on the number of homosexuals marrying (more marry in more anti-homosexual societies).

Third, the consequence of homosexuals marrying in terms of psychological adjustment are not at all obvious: while a low degree of maladjustment or situationally produced problems are apparent in some respondents, it seems clear that there is a high degree of compartmentalisation in the lives of married homosexuals, thus minimising such problems. However, sample bias may account for some of this. If marriage had any effect on their homosexuality, it was to increase its importance.

Finally, a general profile of the reasons for marriage and problems encountered by the married homosexual male, the identifiable sub-types together with the particular characteristics and adaptations they exhibit, has been drawn and discussed at length with regard to married homosexual males. Clinical and counselling implications have been explored with reference to those respondents who remained married, those who became aware of their orientation at different stages, and those whose spouses became aware of this at different stages of the relationship.

Appendix 1
The questionnaire

VICTORIA UNIVERSITY OF WELLINGTON
Department of Psychology
Survey Questionnaire

I would be grateful if you could fill out this questionnaire to assist me with some on-going research. Please accept my assurance that any information collected in the course of this enquiry will remain strictly confidential and will be used for research purposes only. Moreover, the individuals who have collaborated in the project will in no way be identifiable in any thesis which may result. With this assurance, I look forward once more to your cooperation. There are no 'right' or 'wrong' answers: do not discuss, just give your first reaction to each question. You should then complete the questionnaire in about 15 minutes. While you are not required to give your name or any identifying details, it would be of great assistance if you answered as many questions as possible. If this form is not collected, please mail direct to:

Michael Ross, Department of Psychology,
Victoria University, Private Bag,
Wellington, NZ.

1 Age. . . . .

2 How far have you gone in your education? (tick)
   High School . . . .
   U.E. . . . .
   Some University . . . . . .
   Degree. . . . .
   Graduate degree . . . . . .

3 What sort of work do you do for a living: (state below)
   . . . .

4 How would you place your social class? (tick)
   Upper . . . .
   Upper middle . . . .
   Lower middle . . . .
   working. . . . .

5 With whom do you live? (tick)
   Parent(s) . . . .
   Alone . . . .
   Board . . . .
   Flat (Gay) . . . .
   Flat (non-Gay) . . . .
   Wife . . . .
   Other (specify)
   . . . .

6 Were your teenage years spent primarily in: (tick)
   Large city . . . .
   Medium city. . . . .
   Town . . . .
   Country. . . . .

7 Do you at present live in a:
   Large city . . . .
   Medium city. . . . .
   Town . . . .
   Country. . . . .

8 What is your religious background? (state denomination)
   . . . .

9 How 'religious' were your parents?
   very religious . . . .
   somewhat religious . . . .
   not very religious. . . . . .
   not at all religious . . . . .

10 How 'religious' are you?
   very religious . . . .
   somewhat religious . . . .
   not very religious. . . . . .
   not at all religious . . . . .

11 Do your parents or close relatives live in the same city as you?
   yes . . . .
   no . . . .

12 Which of the following homosexual practices have you frequently engaged in?
   mutual masturbation . . .
   full body stimulation . . .
   fellatio . . . .
   anal intercourse (active)
   . . . . . .
   "   "   (passive)
   . . . . . .

13 Do you think of yourself as:
   exclusively homosexual
   . . . . . .
   predominantly homo-sexual
   . . . . . .
   more homosexual than heterosexual
   . . . . . .
   bisexual
   . . . . . .
   more heterosexual than homosexual
   . . . . . .
   predominantly hetero-sexual
   . . . . . .
   exclusively heterosexual
   . . . . . .

149

14 Do you have sex with?
      men only . . . .
      predominantly men . . . .
      more men than women . .
      equal numbers of both . .
      more women than men . .
      predominantly women . .
      women only . . . .

15 Are you at present:
      single and never married .
      have been married but
      not living with your wife

                        . . . . . .
      married and living with
      your wife   . . . . . .

16 If married or previously
    married, how old were you
    when you got married:

    . . . .

17 Did you think of yourself
    as a homosexual:
      before you married . . . .
      after you married . . . . .
      (if separated)
      after you separated . . . .

18 Did your wife know you
    had homosexual tendencies:
      before you married . . . .
      after you married . . . . .
      after you separated . . . .
      never. . . . .

19 How long have (or did) you
    live with your wife?

    . . . .

20 If separated, how long have
    you lived apart?

    . . . .

21 Do you think you have be-
    come as a result of marriage:
      more homosexual . . . . .

21 (cont)
      less homosexual . . . . . .
      about the same . . . .

22 Do you have any children?
    If, so, how many?

    . . . .

23 Are you:
      Married . . . .
      Separated. . . . .
      Divorced . . . .
      Widowed . . . .

24 Did you marry because of:
    (tick appropriate categories)
      Loneliness . . . .
      Pressure from family . . .
      Pressure from girlfriend
                        . . . . . .
      Everyone else was getting
      married   . . . . . .
      You thought your homo-
      sexuality would go if you
      married   . . . . . .
      Advice from someone
      else   . . . . . .
      You wanted children and
      family life   . . . . . .
      You wanted someone to
      look after you (cook,
      tidy, etc.)   . . . . . .
      It seemed the natural
      thing   . . . . . .
      You were worried about
      your feelings to other
      men   . . . . . .
      You wanted a com-
      panion   . . . . . .
      Other (state) . . . . . .

      . . . .
      . . . .

25 When you married, the best things about marriage were: (state) . . . .
. . . .
. . . .

26 When you married, the worst things about marriage were: (state) . . . .
. . . .
. . . .

27 Did your homosexuality become increasingly important to you at any stage of marriage?
   No . . . .
   Yes . . . .

28 If yes, was it a result of:
   Marriage strains. . . . . . .
   Illness/Death of wife
   . . . . . .
   Children grew up. . . . . .
   Period of absence from wife . . . .
   Meeting a particular Gay person. . . . .
   Wife's frigidity . . . .
   Marriage began to 'grow stale'. . . . .
   Couldn't keep homosexual feelings at bay. . . . . . .
   Other (state). . . . .
   . . . .
   . . . .

29 Have you ever thought of re-marrying?
   Yes. . . . .
   No . . . .

30 Do you currently have a homosexual partner?

30 (cont)
   Yes . . . .
   No . . . .

31 Have you ever had a regular homosexual partner?
   Yes. . . . .
   No . . . .

32 If yes, was this after your marriage?
   Yes. . . . .
   No . . . .

33 Have you ever had any regular female partners? (Apart from your wife)
   Yes. . . . .
   No . . . .

34 If yes, was this after your marriage?
   Yes. . . . .
   No . . . .

35 At what age did you first have sexual relations with a male? (state) . . . .

36 At what age did you first have sexual relations with a female? (state) . . . .

37 Indicate the extent to which you agree that the statements below characterise you and your feelings. After reading each statement:

   Circle   if you . .
   SA   Strongly agree
   A   Agree
   ?   Are not sure
   D   Disagree
   SD   Strongly disagree

37 (cont)

I feel that I have a number of good qualities.	SA A ? D SD
Being homosexual is something that is completely beyond one's control.	SA A ? D SD
Homosexuals are usually superior in many ways to non-homosexuals.	SA A ? D SD
I take a positive attitude towards myself.	SA A ? D SD
No one is going to care much what happens to you, when you get right down to it.	SA A ? D SD
What consenting adults do in private is nobody's business, as long as they don't hurt other people.	SA A ? D SD
If you don't watch out for yourself, people will take advantage of you.	SA A ? D SD
Human nature is really cooperative.	SA A ? D SD
I look effeminate.	SA A ? D SD
Most people can be trusted.	SA A ? D SD
Homosexuality may best be described as an illness.	SA A ? D SD
On the whole, I am satisfied with myself.	SA A ? D SD
I am not as happy as others seem to be.	SA A ? D SD
I prefer to pass by friends or people I know but have not seen for a long time unless they speak to me first.	SA A ? D SD
I feel that I'm a person of worth, at least on an equal plane with others.	SA A ? D SD
I feel that it is easier for me to talk to male homosexuals than to male heterosexuals.	SA A ? D SD
I feel it is easier for me to talk to male heterosexuals than to female heterosexuals.	SA A ? D SD
I tend to behave effeminately when in the straight world.	SA A ? D SD
All in all, I am inclined to feel that I'm a failure.	SA A ? D SD
I do not like to associate socially with a person who has a reputation (among heterosexuals) of being homosexual.	SA A ? D SD
I do not care who knows about my homosexuality.	SA A ? D SD
I have a harder time than other people in gaining friends.	SA A ? D SD
When I was a teenager, I was unpopular with girls.	SA A ? D SD
I wish I were not homosexual.	SA A ? D SD

37 (cont)

I would not want to give up my homosexuality even if I could.	SA A ? D SD
I certainly feel useless at times.	SA A ? D SD
I have a harder time than other people in making conversation.	SA A ? D SD
I often find myself 'putting on an act' to impress people.	SA A ? D SD
People have made fun of me because I am a homosexual.	SA A ? D SD
Homosexuals and heterosexuals are basically different in more ways than simple sexual preference.	SA A ? D SD
I am able to do things as well as most other people.	SA A ? D SD
Most people are inclined to look after themselves.	SA A ? D SD
I feel that I don't have enough friends.	SA A ? D SD
Usually it is the most unethical, immoral or hypocritical members of heterosexual society that are most likely to condemn homosexuals.	SA A ? D SD
I have noticed that my ideas about myself seem to change very quickly.	SA A ? D SD
I feel 'closer' to a heterosexual of my own social class than to a homosexual who is of a much lower class.	SA A ? D SD
I feel that nothing, or almost nothing, can change the opinion I currently hold of myself.	SA A ? D SD
It would not bother me if I had children who were homosexual.	SA A ? D SD
I am easily embarrassed.	SA A ? D SD
Some days I have a very good opinion of myself; other days I have a very poor opinion of myself.	SA A ? D SD
There have been times when I felt as though I was going to have a nervous breakdown.	SA A ? D SD
In general, I feel in low spirits most of the time.	SA A ? D SD
I get a lot of fun out of life.	SA A ? D SD
There is nothing immoral about being homosexual.	SA A ? D SD
A person is born homosexual or heterosexual.	SA A ? D SD
I often feel downcast and dejected.	SA A ? D SD
I am probably responsible for the fact I am homosexual.	SA A ? D SD

37 (cont)

On the whole, I think I am quite a happy person.	SA A ? D SD
Homosexuality tends to have a negative effect on society at large.	SA A ? D SD
Homosexuality may best be described as a mental illness.	SA A ? D SD
I tend to be a rather shy person.	SA A ? D SD
I would not mind being seen in public with a person who has the reputation (among heterosexuals) of being homosexual.	SA A ? D SD
I wish I could have more respect for myself.	SA A ? D SD
I often feel very self-conscious.	SA A ? D SD
I tend to behave effeminately when I'm with other homosexuals.	SA A ? D SD
I feel I do not have much to be proud of.	SA A ? D SD
At times I feel I am no good at all.	SA A ? D SD
I often feel ill at ease when I'm in the presence of others.	SA A ? D SD

38 Of the following people, check how many suspect or know you are homosexual:

	All	Most	More than half	Half	Less than half	Only a few	None
Heterosexuals who you know	....	....	....	....	....	....	....
Male heterosexual friends	....	....	....	....	....	....	....
Female heterosexual friends	....	....	....	....	....	....	....
Aunts and uncles	....	....	....	....	....	....	....
Neighbours	....	....	....	....	....	....	....
Work associates	....	....	....	....	....	....	....
People you suspect or know are homosexual	....	....	....	....	....	....	....

39 Do any of the following people know or suspect that you are homo-
    sexual? If they are deceased, tick whether they did know or
    suspect. If you have no such relationship, tick 'Not applicable'.

	Definitely know	Probably suspect	Do not know	Not applicable
Your mother	....	....	....	....
Your father	....	....	....	....
Brother(s)	....	....	....	....
Sister(s)	....	....	....	....
Best heterosexual friend (same sex)	....	....	....	•......
Best heterosexual friend (opposite sex)	....	....	....	....
Your employer	....	....	....	....

40 How do you think each of the following persons would react
    (or has reacted) to finding out that you are homosexual? (√
    for has, X for would).

	Accepting	Understanding	Tolerant	Intolerant	Rejecting	Not applicable
Mother	....	....	....	....	....	....
Father	....	....	....	....	....	....
Brother(s)	....	....	....	....	....	....
Sister(s)	....	....	....	....	....	....
Most of aunts/uncles	....	....	....	....	....	....
Best heterosexual friend (same sex)	....	....	....	....	....	....
Most other heterosexual friends	....	....	....	....	....	....
Best heterosexual friend (opposite sex)	....	....	....	....	....	....
Wife	....	....	....	....	....	....
Most of work associates	....	....	....	....	....	....
Employer	....	....	....	....	....	....
Most of neighbours	....	....	....	....	....	....
Heterosexuals in general	....	....	....	....	....	....

41 How important do you personally think each of the following is: (tick the space as close to, or as far from, 'Very important' as characterises your feelings).

	Very Important					Not at all important
Formal religion	....	....	....	....	....	....
Traditional morality	....	....	....	....	....	....
Conformity in general	....	....	....	....	....	....

42 All of us value the opinions of some people more than others. How important is it to you that each of the following persons has (or had) a 'good' opinion of you? Tick the space as close to, or as far from, 'Very important' as characterises your feelings:

	Very important					Not at all important
Mother	....	....	....	....	....	....
Father	....	....	....	....	....	....
Brother(s)	....	....	....	....	....	....
Sister(s)	....	....	....	....	....	....
Most of aunts/uncles	....	....	....	....	....	....
Best heterosexual friend (same sex)	....	....	....	....	....	....
Best heterosexual friend (opposite sex)	....	....	....	....	....	....
Most other heterosexual friends	....	....	....	....	....	....
Wife	....	....	....	....	....	....
Most of work associates	....	....	....	....	....	....
Employer	....	....	....	....	....	....
Most of your neighbours	....	....	....	....	....	....
Heterosexuals in general	....	....	....	....	....	....
Best homosexual friends	....	....	....	....	....	....
Homosexuals in general	....	....	....	....	....	....

43 To what degree do you think homosexuality violates the following:

	Very much	Somewhat	Not much	Not at all
Formal religion	....	....	....	....
Traditional morality	....	....	....	....
Conformity in general	....	....	....	....

156

In the following questions, choose the alternative that best characterises your situation. Circle the number opposite the answer you choose.

44 Of all your friends, how many (to your knowledge) are heterosexual?

All	1
Most	2
More than half	3
About half	4
Less than half	5
Only a few	6
None	7

45 How socially active were you in heterosexual circles when you first began to really view yourself as homosexual?

Very active	1
Somewhat active	2
Not too active	3
Not active at all	4

46 How many close relationships did you have with heterosexuals when you first began to view yourself as homosexual?

Many	1
Some	2
Very few	3
None	4

47 How popular were you in heterosexual circles when you first began to view yourself as homosexual?

Quite popular	1
Reasonably popular	2
Not very popular	3
Not at all popular	4

48 At the present, how many close relationships do you have with heterosexuals (other than family)?

Many	1
Some	2
Very few	3
None	4

49 At the present, how socially active are you in heterosexual circles?

Very active	1
Somewhat active	2
Not too active	3
Not active at all	4

50 At the present, how popular are you in heterosexual circles?

Quite popular	1
Reasonably popular	2
Not very popular	3
Not popular at all	4

51 From how many heterosexuals do you try to conceal your homosexuality?

All	1
Most	2
More than half	3
About half	4
Less than half	5
Only a few	6
None	7

52 Have there been problems on any job you've had because people suspected or knew you were homosexual?

No	1

52 (cont)

    Yes, very few   2

    Yes, to some degree   3

    Yes, a lot   4

53 Would there be problems at work if people found out?

    No   1

    Yes, very few   2

    Yes, to some degree   3

    Yes, a lot   4

    Most know already   5

54 Have you ever lost a job because your homosexuality became known?

    Yes, more than once   1

    Yes, once   2

    No   3

55 Have you ever been labelled a homosexual?

    Yes more than once   1

    Yes, once   2

    No   3

56 If 'Yes': Does this bother you? If 'No': Would this bother you?

    Yes, a lot   1

    Yes, somewhat   2

    Yes, but not much   3

    No   4

57 Has suspicion or knowledge of your homosexuality adversely affected your social relationships?

    Yes, a lot   1

    Yes, somewhat   2

    Yes, but not much   3

    No   4

58 Do you think people are likely to break off a social

58 (cont)

relationship with someone they suspect is homosexual?

    Yes, most   1

    Yes, many   2

    Yes, a few   3

    No   4

59 Do you think people are likely to make life difficult for people they suspect are homosexual?

    Yes, most   1

    Yes, many   2

    Yes, a few   3

    No   4

60 Has life been made difficult for you because someone knew or suspected you were homosexual?

    Yes, very much   1

    Yes, somewhat   2

    Yes, to some degree   3

    No   4

61 How do you think most people feel about homo-sexuals?

    Disgusted or repelled   1

    Dislike homosexuals   2

    A 'live and let live' attitude   3

    Like homosexuals   4

62 What proportion of your leisure time is spent socia-lising with homosexuals?

    Most   1

    More than half   2

    About half   3

    Less than half   4

    A very small amount   5

62 (cont)

  None   6

63 How many of your friends are homosexual?

  All   1
  Most   2
  More than half   3
  About half   4
  Less than half   5
  A very small number   6
  None   7

64 For how long have you had mostly homosexual friends?

  Have never had mostly homosexual friends   1
  Only in the past   2
  Past 6 months or less   3
  Between 6 months and a year   4
  Between 1 and 2 years   5
  Longer than 2 years   6

65 Which category best describes your social situation among homosexuals?

  Not really known among them   1
  Not part of the group   2
  Accepted   3
  Well accepted   4
  Popular socially   5

66 How often do you usually frequent homosexual bars or clubs?

  More than once a week   1
  About once a week   2
  About once a fortnight   3
  About once a month   4
  Every few months   5
  Almost never   6

66 (cont)

  Never   7

67 Have you ever danced with another male?

  Yes, often   1
  Yes, sometimes   2
  Yes, once   3
  Never   4

68 Has kissing been part of your homosexual practice?

  Yes, often   1
  Yes, sometimes   2
  Yes, once   3
  Never   4

69 Have you ever appeared dressed in women's clothing in front of others?

  Yes, often   1
  Yes, sometimes   2
  Yes, once   3
  Never   4

70 At the present, are another homosexual and yourself limiting your sexual relationships primarily to each other?

  No   1
  Yes, for less than a month   2
  Yes, from 1-6 months   3
  Yes, from 6 months to a year   4
  Yes, for more than a year   5

71 At some time in the past, did you and another homosexual limit your sexual relationships primarily to each other?

  No   1

71 (cont)

    Yes   2

72 What do you think most homosexuals that know you think of you?

    Think well of me   1

    Think fairly well of me   2

    Are neutral to me   3

    Think fairly poorly of me   4

    Think very poorly of me   5

    Don't associate with enough to answer this   6

73 What do you think most heterosexuals you associate with think of you?

    Think well of me   1

    Think fairly well of me   2

    Are neutral to me   3

    Think fairly poorly of me   4

    Think very poorly of me   5

74 Even though it may be difficult please specify the number of people you consider to be close friends: (state) . . . .

75 Of these, how many are homosexual: (state) . . . .

76 Even though it may be difficult, in your answers to these questions, try to provide numbers.

    In the last 6 months, how many females have you had sexual relations with?

    . . . .

76 (cont)

    In the last 6 months, how many males have you had sexual relations with?

    . . . .

    At what age did you have your first heterosexual experience?

    . . . .

    At what age did you have your first homosexual experience?

    . . . .

77 Has anyone ever suggested that you receive psychiatric treatment of your homosexuality?

    Yes, several   1

    Yes, one   2

    No   3

78 Regarding your homosexuality, have you ever visited a psychiatrist?

    Yes   1

    No   2

Have you ever received psychiatric treatment?

    Yes   1

    No   2

Are you currently receiving psychiatric treatment?

    Yes   1

    No   2

If 'No', would you like to have psychiatric treatment?

    Yes   1

    No   2

Have you ever had psychiatric treatment for reasons other than your homo-

78 (cont)
sexuality?

Yes	1
No	2

79 Do you ever find that on one day you have one opinion of yourself and on another day you have a different opinion?

Yes, often	1
Yes, sometimes	2
Yes, rarely	3
No	4

80 Do you worry about possible exposure of your homosexuality?

A great deal	1
Somewhat	2
Very little	3
Not at all	4

81 Does the opinion you have of yourself tend to change a great deal?

Yes, a great deal	1
Yes, somewhat	2
Yes, rarely	3
No	4

82 Does knowing that you are homosexual make you feel guilty, depressed, anxious or ashamed?

Yes, a great deal	1
Yes, somewhat	2
Yes, rarely	3
No	4

83 At the present, do you ever experience shame, guilt, or anxiety after homosexual sex?

83 (cont)

Nearly always	1
Often	2
Not very much	3
Never	4

84 Did you feel guilt or shame after your first homosexual experience?

Yes, a lot	1
Yes, some	2
Yes, but very little	3
No	4

85 Do you feel lonely?

Never	1
Seldom	2
Often	3
Very often	4

86 Overall, how would you say you feel these days? Are you:

Very happy	1
Pretty happy	2
Not too happy	3
Very unhappy	4

87 For how long have you thought of yourself as being homosexual (or partly homosexual)?

Never	1
Only in the past	2
Less than a year	3
Less than 3 years	4
3 to 5 years	5
6 to 9 years	6
Over 10 years	7

88   How often do the following things happen to you?

	Nearly all the time	Often	Not very much	Never
1 Do you ever have any trouble getting to sleep?	....	....	....	....
2 Have you ever been bothered by nervousness, feeling tense and fidgety?	....	....	....	....
3 Are you ever troubled by headaches or pains in the head?	....	....	....	....
4 Do you have loss of appetite?	....	....	....	....
5 How often are you bothered by having an upset stomach?	....	....	....	....
6 Do you find it difficult to get up in the morning?	....	....	....	....
7 Have you ever been bothered by shortness of breath when you were not working hard?	....	....	....	....
8 Have you ever been bothered by your heart beating hard?	....	....	....	....
9 Do you ever drink more than you should?	....	....	....	....
10 Have you ever had spells of dizziness?	....	....	....	....
11 Are you ever bothered by nightmares?	....	....	....	....
12 Do you tend to lose weight when you have something important bothering you?	....	....	....	....
13 Do your hands ever tremble enough to bother you?	....	....	....	....
14 Are you troubled by your hands sweating so that you feel damp and clammy?	....	....	....	....
15 Have there been times when you couldn't take care of things because you just couldn't get going?	....	....	....	....

89   Which of the following do you favour, approve of, or believe in?
       Circle 'Y' (Yes) or 'N' (No). If absolutely uncertain, circle '?'.
       There are no right or wrong answers; just give your first reaction.

Death penalty	Y ? N	Electronic music	Y ? N
Evolution theory	Y ? N	Chastity	Y ? N
School uniforms	Y ? N	Fluoridation	Y ? N
Striptease shows	Y ? N	Royalty	Y ? N
Sabbath observance	Y ? N	Woman judges	Y ? N
Hippies	Y ? N	Conventional clothing	Y ? N
Patriotism	Y ? N	Trade unions	Y ? N
Modern art	Y ? N	Apartheid	Y ? N

89 (cont)

Self-denial	Y ? N		Nudist camps	Y ? N	
Working mothers	Y ? N		Church authority	Y ? N	
Masculine superiority	Y ? N		Disarmament	Y ? N	
Birth control	Y ? N		Censorship	Y ? N	
Military drill	Y ? N		Workers' strikes	Y ? N	
Co-education	Y ? N		Birching	Y ? N	
Divine law	Y ? N		Racially mixed marriage	Y ? N	
Socialism	Y ? N		Strict rules	Y ? N	
White superiority	Y ? N		Jazz	Y ? N	
Cousin marriage	Y ? N		Straitjackets	Y ? N	
Missionaries	Y ? N		Recognition of China	Y ? N	
Student demonstrators	Y ? N		Peacetime conscription	Y ? N	
Security intelligence service	Y ? N		Divorce	Y ? N	
Legalised abortion	Y ? N		Austere prisons	Y ? N	
Empire-building	Y ? N		Coloured immigration	Y ? N	
Student pranks	Y ? N		Bible truth	Y ? N	
Licensing laws	Y ? N		Free medical treatment	Y ? N	

If there is anything you wish to further explain or elaborate on, please do so below. Thank you again for your cooperation.

Appendix 2
Structure of the questionnaire

Factor analysis was carried out in order to check the original questionnaire scales: the original questionnaire of Weinberg and Williams (1974, pp. 293-306) was adapted to both the purpose of this research and to this country. Such additions and deletions as occur are minor and often only changes of detail. Rather than start from the beginning and design and pre-test a new questionnaire, it was decided to adapt the most suitable questionnaire already in use, both to save time, expense and unnecessary duplication of research, and to provide a better comparison with the work of Weinberg and Williams. Questions 1 to 4 of the research instrument are adaptations at a simpler level of questions 117 to 130 of the original questionnaire. Since most of these questions dealt with occupation, and job satisfaction, they were edited, or deleted if they asked for detail which the respondents in the present sample, who were very reluctant to put down anything which could possibly identify them, would not wish to give. Questions 5 to 13 are questions 113, 115, 131 to 141 from the original questionnaire. Again, for ease of administration, some questions were edited, or deleted, because they were inappropriate, for example questions on race, membership of societies, such as the Mattachine, and area of a city in which one lived. Question 14, the behavioural Kinsey Scale, was added, and question 15 is the original question 97 edited.

Questions 16 to 36 of the research instrument are additional to the original questionnaire, and designed to explore particularly the situation of the married homosexual.

Questions 37 to 88 are questions 1 to 94, 100 to 111 of the original questionnaire. Question 89 is the Wilson-Patterson Conservatism scale (Wilson, 1973). None of the questions of the original questionnaire, apart from those asking for demographic or background data, were altered in any way, and those deleted either concerned societies or situations specific to countries other than New Zealand and Australia, or went into unnecessary detail and were collapsed into one question. Some of the latter category were avoided because of undue specificity which could have identified respondents.

Weinberg and Williams have grouped some of the attitudinal and personality-based items into scales on the basis of face-valid relationships, and items in the scales interpreted in conjunction with other items in the same scale. While items were in the present study interpreted individually, analysis has also been carried out on the scales as a whole. In order to test the assumptions behind the seventeen scales, nine of which appear to be personality-based, a Factor Analysis was carried out on them.

Factor Analysis (varimax rotation) of the fifty-eight personality-related items of the Weinberg and Williams scales gives seventeen factors. While some of these do not correspond exactly with the scales which Weinberg and Williams have designated as measuring particular personality traits, there is a certain degree of correspondence. In cases where factors which do not measure particular previously nominated personality variables occur, they are discussed with particular reference to the sample.

Factor I appears to be a general one measuring depression and uneasiness in respondents, and corresponds fairly exactly with the 'depression' scale of Weinberg and Williams. Underlying the 'depression' scale is a tendency for a low opinion of oneself and seeing oneself in a very unfavourable light, particularly in interaction with others. From the loading of the item 'Homosexuality may be described as a mental illness' (.56) it would appear that the depression is strongly related to homosexuality. There is a little doubt that depression is being measured by the original 'depression' scale, since all items of the scale have factor loadings of > .30. However, there are a number of items from the scale in the original questionnaire which purported to measure 'interpersonal awkwardness', suggesting that respondents who see themselves as having difficulty with interpersonal relations are in fact stating this as an expression of depression. Thus, the scale purporting to measure 'interpersonal awkwardness' splits into two factors, one with depression-related variables and the second, Factor V.

Factor II measures the trait of overtness or openness about one's orientation. The scale 'obviousness of homosexuality' was created in the present study from a group of items which were taken individually by Weinberg and Williams. All these items have a high (> .30) loading on Factor II, along with the item measuring passing. Clearly, there is a meaningful group of items which indicate overtness about orientation, including some stability of opinion of one's orientation as indicated by the loading on the item Q37 (35). Characterising overtness are such factors of behaviour as stereotyped homosexual behaviour, and 'flighty', changeable, moody behaviour, tying overtness in strongly with the public stereotyped image of the homosexual.

Factor III corresponds closely with the 'self-acceptance' scale of Weinberg and Williams, with six of the ten items with high loadings on Factor III being from this scale. From the items with the highest loadings, it would appear that this factor measures not so much the general factor of self-acceptance as that sort of self-acceptance which could be described as personal optimism and feelings of personal worth. Those items which were on the 'interpersonal awkwardness' scale, which appear with high loadings on Factor III, relate to feeling optimistic about interpersonal relationships.

Factor IV largely corresponds to the scale said to measure 'faith in others', on the original questionnaire. Four of the seven items with high loadings on this factor are from the original scale, and seem to be measuring a general paranoia, with some projection of trust in others to oneself, as evidenced by Q37 (12). Particularly, there is a relationship between acceptance of one's orientation and this generalised paranoia, with the assumption appearing to be that if the individual can accept his orientation, others will also. The new Factor

IV scale would appear to be related to projected expectations of reaction to homosexuality, and if one does describe this as 'faith in others', it seems to be faith in others' reactions to homosexuality being positive.

Factor V bears some relationship to the original scale labelled 'interpersonal awkwardness', although only in a very limited sense. This factor measures not so much interpersonal awkwardness but a sense of inadequacy, shyness or introversion in a general sense, almost a reverse of Factor III although less specific.

Factor VI tends to correspond to some extent with the original scale 'stability of self-concept', measuring one's stability of opinion and sureness of oneself, particularly when concerned with ability to mix with others and manage one's social life. It also contains a component of psychological stability as can be seen in items Q37 (33 and 41), which refer to reactions to supportive and coping mechanisms. While in some respects similar to Factor III it deals with stability of acceptance rather than acceptance itself.

Factor VII is primarily a composite factor, taking items from the three original scales dealing with views of respondents to homosexuality, especially those which reflect on its acceptability to the respondent. It is perhaps similar to a self-acceptance scale referring only to one's orientation. The main component seems to be almost pride in, rather than acceptance of, the respondent's homosexuality: there is a strong implication from all the items with high loadings that homosexuality is an acceptable and positive life-style.

Factor VIII measures a different type of homosexual commitment, one which is socially based rather than internally based, as in Factor VII. The basis of the factor is the view that it is easier to relate to males and particularly male homosexuals in preference to others, and that although the respondents may feel they have few friends it is difficult to communicate with people with whom they have little in common or cannot identify with.

Factor IX could broadly be described as perception of social reaction to homosexuality. Items stressed include those suggesting that people are not going to worry about individual feelings and that respondents would go out of their way to avoid being labelled homosexual. There is a tendency to feel that it is not only the hypocritical members of society who condemn homosexuals, and for the respondents to think that their orientation is their own responsibility to some extent. This factor could be described as very similar to the general construct scale referred to as 'putative peer and societal reaction' used earlier in this paper.

Factor X corresponds closely to the original scale labelled 'conception of responsibility for homosexuality', the items with very high loadings (> .50) all being from this scale. The other items with high loadings on this factor reflect lack of depression, making this a factor of non-acceptance of moral responsibility for the respondent's orientation and relative optimism of outlook.

Factor XI is similarly a scale measuring an aspect of conception of homosexuality, but stressing self-acceptance of responsibility for homosexuality, unlike Factor VII. Factor XI has high loadings on the items from the original scale of 'conception of responsibility for homosexuality' in much the same pattern as Factor X, but includes two items from the original 'self-acceptance' scale, giving a pattern which makes this factor one measuring acceptance of responsibility and positive self-image of oneself as a homosexual. In this way it is a personalisation of Factor VII.

At this stage, there occur a number of factors which have very few items with high loadings, in some cases only two items per factor. Since it is difficult to construct a personality factor on two items, discussion of factors has been kept to a minimum, as some very similar factors begin to emerge which cannot be adequately differentiated from one another and the extant factors. Given the relatively small sample, it is possible that beyond this point there is little purpose in discussing factors which could have little meaning. There is some possibility that factor fission may have occurred, but without further analysis this cannot be ascertained.

Using Kaiser's criterion (cut-off at the latent root, i.e., eigen value, of 1) seventeen factors are extracted. However, Child (1970) notes that, when more than fifty variables are used, too many factors tend to be taken out. Cattell's (1966) scree test, however, when applied, gives a cut-off point of

Factor IX, the point where the curve straightens out. Only one factor past this point, Factor XIV makes any sense: it is essentially the original scale 'conception of homosexuality as normal', with one other item included, which indicates some identification with other male homosexuals in addition to seeing homosexuality as a 'normal behaviour'.

From the Factor Analysis, it can be seen that there is a fair degree of correspondence between the original scales suggested using alpha coefficients (Weinberg and Williams, 1974). However, while each of the original scales shows a predominance of items in one particular factor, some items which were assumed to measure a particular trait are demonstrated to measure another, totally different, trait, a good example being the original scale 'interpersonal awkwardness' which split between three factors, I, III and V. Nevertheless, component analysis does show clearly which aspects of the traits are being measured by the scales used. Since the in-depth analysis of the questionnaires was carried out by individual item rather than primarily by scale, this does not affect the results or conclusions, but adds depth to the interpretation of those scales which showed significant difference between groups. The fact that, of the nine original scales which contributed items to the component analysis, none showed more than a significant trend ($p < .10 > .05$) between any of the groups analysed, is probably due to the fact that none of the original scales was a 'pure' measure, but contained elements of other factors in their computation, apart from the scale 'conception of homosexuality as normal', Factor XIV, which gave one result as significant on the chi-square analysis.

While it would be interesting to recompute the scales as the factor analysis would suggest, it would require a great amount of additional work. Weinberg and Williams, while organising items into scales, did not actually compute scales, but compared items within scales. Clearly, placing items into scales gives a greater possibility of demonstrating the hypotheses, as has been shown with the remaining eight scales not based on personality factors, such as 'being known about' and 'expected societal reaction'.

Nevertheless, the research instrument, even without the

factor analysis to confirm the grouping of items into scales, lends itself, by an analysis in terms of face validity of items individually, to in-depth analysis of attitudes and psychological factors affecting the respondents. While the Factor Analysis also gives greater depth of interpretation to the computed scales and stresses the aspects which are actually measured rather than those which it is assumed are measured, with further testing the Weinberg and Williams questionnaire should be able to be used as a personality measure as well as measuring attitudes and psychological factors on the basis of single items, a procedure which limits hypothesis testing as well as interpretation.

Table A2.1 **Varimax rotated factor matrix, Q37(1) to (58): factor loadings for items**

Factor I			Factor II		Factor III		Factor IV	
37.7	-	32	37.9	69	37.4	- 50	37.7	40
13		41	18	42	12	- 43	8	43
26	-	46	21	- 56	13	30	10	82
27		31	29	85	15	- 65	12	64
33		32	35	- 58	22	66	24	39
39		49	41	38	27	34	32	30
40	-	44	42	32	31	- 77	47	43
42		47	55	31	52	52		
43		73			53	- 42		
46		78			57	- 34		
50	-	56						
51		43						
54		73						
58		72						

Factor V			Factor VI		Factor VII		Factor VIII	
37.7	-	33	37.28	71	37.1	52	37.14	36
14		52	33	34	11	56	16	49
18		45	37	- 79	23	37	17	83
19	-	63	40	- 44	24	37	22	34
36		71	41	35	25	81	34	40
39		59	51	40				
57		42						

Factor IX			Factor X			Factor XI			Factor XIV	
37.2	-	31	37.2	72		37.1	45		37.3	77
5	-	64	8	33		2	32		11	32
18		49	45	82		8	40		16	- 50
20		76	48	35		44	85		30	69
34		45				47	44		47	36
35	-	31							50	35
51		43								

(Decimal points have been omitted from the factor loadings.)

Table A2.2 **Breakdown of questionnaire by scale**

Scale	Question Nos
Self acceptance	37 (1,4,12,15,19,26,53,56,57)
Stability of self-concept	37 (35,37,40,79,81)
Depression	37 (42,43,46,48,86)
Psychosomatic symptoms	88
Anxiety regarding homosexuality	82,83
Interpersonal awkwardness	37 (14,22,27,39,51,54,58)
Faith in others	37 (5,7,8,10,32)
Loneliness	37 (33),85
Psychiatric experience	78
Conception of responsibility for homosexuality	37 (2,45,47)
Obviousness (as a homosexual)	37 (9,18,29,55)
Conception of homosexuality as normal	37 (3,11,30,38,50)
Passing as heterosexual	37 (20,21,52),51
Homosexual commitment	37 (24,25)
Being known about (others)	38
Being known about (family)	39
Dependence on others	42
Putative societal/peer reaction	40,53,61,58,59,72,73
Conception of traditional values	41
Perceived breach of traditional values	43
Social involvement with heterosexuals	44,48,49
Coming out: social situation	45,46,47
Acculturation	67,68,69
Homosexual relations	70,71

All questions not specifically referred to as part of a scale were analysed on their own. Some questions which do form part of a scale were also separately analysed.

Appendix 3
Tables of results

Table A3.1 **Significance levels, items by married and separated R's**

Item Q.No.	χ^2 P	Item Q.No.	χ^2 P	Scale	χ^2 P=
5	**	39.5	**	Depression	.09
6	*	39.6	**	Anxiety regarding	
7	**	39.7	*	homosexuality	.07
9	*	40.1	+	Loneliness	.06
13	**	40.3	*	Passing	.005
14	**	40.4	+	Conception of	
23	**	40.6	*	homosexuality	
24	+	40.7	+	(responsibility)	.06
25	+	40.8	*	Being known	
26	+	41.1	+	about (family)	.005
30	*	42.3	*	Being known	
31	+	42.5	+	about (others)	.03
37.1	+	52	+	Expected societal	
37.6	*	56	*	reaction	.006
37.19	**	58	+		
37.22	*	62	**		
37.38	+	63	**		
37.44	*	64	**		
37.45	*	65	**		
37.46	*	66	+		
37.52	+	67	**		
37.56	*	76.1	**		
38.1	+	78.1	*		
38.2	*	78.2	*		
38.3	**	78.5	*		
38.5	+	80	*		
38.7	**	83	**		
39.1	*	88.2	+		
39.2	+	88.12	+		
39.3	*	88.13	*		

$+ p < .075$ $* p < .05$ $** p < .01$

Table A3.2 **Significance levels on items, married by unmarried samples**

Item Q.No.	χ^2 P	Item Q.No.	χ^2 P	Scale	χ^2 P=
5	**	40.10	*	Psychosomatic	
6	**	40.11	**	symptoms	.09
7	*	40.12	**	Anxiety regarding	
13	**	40.13	**	homosexuality	.03
14	**	42.4	*	Passing	.005
37.10	*	42.10	+	Conception of	
37.17	*	44	*	homosexuality as	
37.30	*	45	**	normal	.004
37.49	*	47	*	Being known	
38.1	*	49	+	about (family)	.002
38.2	*	51	**	Being known	
38.3	**	53	**	about (others)	.01
38.4	**	56	+	Expected societal	
38.5	*	58	**	reaction	.001
38.6	+	59	**	Dependence on	
38.7	+	61	**	others	.08
39.1	+	65	+	Faith in others	.009
39.2	*	66	*		
39.3	**	70	*		
39.4	*	72	+		
39.5	**	79	*		
39.6	**	81	*		
39.7	*	82	+		
40.1	*	83	*		
40.2	**	84	**		
40.3	**	88.1	+		
40.5	*	88.2	**		
40.6	*	88.4	**		
40.7	**	88.5	+		
40.8	+	88.12	+		

+ p < .075   * p < .05   ** p < .01

Table A3.3 **Significance levels on items, high by low on Kinsey Behaviour Scale**

Item Q.No.	$\chi^2\ P$	Scale	$\chi^2\ P =$
4	*	Interpersonal awkwardness	.09
7	+	Anxiety regarding homosexuality	.003
15	**	Obviousness of homosexuality	.006
33	**	Loneliness	.07
37.1	*	Passing	.006
37.5	*	Conception of homosexuality	
37.15	*	(responsibility)	.07
37.21	+	Conception of homosexuality	
37.45	*	as normal	.02
37.56	*	Being known about (others)	.07
40.6	**	Being known about (family)	.07
40.7	+	Dependence on others	.07
41.3	+		
42.1	**		
42.2	*		
43.3	+		
56	**		
60	*		
63	*		
67	+		
68	+		
71	*		
88.11	**		
88.12	**		
88.13	**		

+ p < .075   * p < .05   ** p < .01

Table A3.4 **Significance levels on items, by time of discovery of orientation**

Item Q.No.	χ^2 P	Scale	χ^2 P =
8	+	Stability of self-concept	.06
11	+	Being known about (family)	.001
18	**	Expected societal reaction	.06
21	**	Dependence on others	.03
22	+		
27	**		
29	*		
36	**		
37.32	+		
37.36	*		
37.40	+		
38.7	*		
39.4	*		
39.6	**		
40.3	*		
41.1	**		
41.2	**		
44	+		
47	+		
60	*		
70	**		
74	**		
78.2	*		
87	*		

$+ \; p < .075$ $* \; p < .05$ $** \; p < .01$

Table A3.5 Significance levels, items by time of wife's discovery of orientation

Item Q.No.	χ^2 P	Item Q.No.	χ^2 P	Scale	χ^2 P=
13	+	40(2)	**	Obviousness of	
17	**	40(4)	**	homosexuality	.05
22	*	40(5)	+	Passing	.002
23	+	40(6)	**	Being known about	
27	*	40(7)	+	(others)	.03
37(21)	**	40(8)	*	Being known about	
37(29)	+	40(9)	**	(family)	.005
38(1)	**	40(10)	**	Expected societal	
38(2)	**	40(11)	**	reaction	.002
38(3)	**	42(8)	+		
38(4)	**	51	*		
38(6)	*	53	*		
39(1)	**	55	**		
39(2)	**	60	*		
39(3)	*	63	+		
39(4)	*	67	*		
39(5)	**	77	*		
39(6)	78(1)	**			
39(7)					

+ p $<$ .075   * p $<$ .05   ** p $<$ .01

Table A3.6 **Significance levels, items by score on expected societal reaction scale**

Item Q.No.	χ^2 P	Item Q.No.	χ^2 P	Scale	χ^2 P=
4	**	40(3)	**	Anxiety regarding	
5	**	40(4)	**	homosexuality	.008
6	+	40(5)	*	Loneliness	.06
13	*	40(6)	**	Passing	.0005
14	**	40(7)	**	Homosexual	
15	**	40(8)	**	commitment	.095
16	+	40(10)	**		
18	**	40(11)	**		
21	+	40(12)	**		
23	*	40(13)	**		
37(1)	*	43(3)	*		
37(6)	+	44	+		
37(11)	**	51	*		
37(18)	+	53	*		
37(23)	+	55	+		
37(30)	**	56	+		
37(31)	*	57	*		
37(46)	**	58	**		
37(56)	**	59	**		
38(1)	**	61	**		
38(2)	*	63	**		
38(3)	**	65	**		
38(4)	+	67	*		
38(5)	*	68	*		
38(7)	*	78(2)	+		
39(1)	*	80	*		
39(2)	+	81	+		
39(3)	**	83	*		
39(5)	**	84	*		
39(6)	**	85	+		
40(1)	**	88(11)	*		
40(2)	**				

+ p < .075   * p < .05   ** p < .01

References

Adorno, T. W., Frenkl-Brunswick, E., Levinson, D. J. and Sandford, R. N., *The Authoritiarian Personality*, New York: Harper, 1950.

Asch, S. E., 'Effects of group pressure upon the modification and distortion of judgements', in Swanson, G. E., Newcomb, J. M., and Hartley, E. L. (eds), *Readings in Social Psychology*, New York: Holt, Rinehart and Winston, 1952.

Bandura, A., Ross, D. and Ross, S. A., 'A comparative test of the status envy, social power, and the secondary reinforcement theories of identification learning', *Journal of Abnormal and Social Psychology*, 1963, 67, 527-34.

Bell, A. P. and Weinberg, M. S., *Homosexualities: A Study of Diversity among Men and Women*, Melbourne: Macmillan, 1978.

Bem, S. L., 'The measurement of psychological androgyny', *Journal of Consulting and Clinical Psychology*, 1974, 42, 155-62.

Bem, S. L., 'On the utility of alternative procedures for assessing psychological androgyny', *Journal of Consulting and Clinical Psychology*, 1977, 45, 196-205.

Breger, L., 'Conformity as a function of the ability to express hostility', *Journal of Personality*, 1963, 31, 247-57.

Byrne, D., *An introduction to personality* (2nd ed.), Englewood Cliffs: Prentice-Hall, 1974.

Cattell, R. B., *Handbook of Multivariate Experimental Psychology*, Chicago: Rand McNally, 1966.

Child, D., *The Essentials of Factor Analysis*, London: Holt, Rinehart & Winston, 1970.

Churchill, W., *Homosexual Behaviour among Males: A Cross-Cultural and Cross-Species Investigation*, Englewood Cliffs: Prentice-Hall, 1967.

Coleman, E., 'Bisexual and gay men in heterosexual marriage: conflicts and resolutions in therapy', *Journal of Homosexuality*, 1982, 7 (2 & 3), 93-103.

Cory, D. W. and LeRoy, J. P., *The Homosexual and his Society*, New York: Citadel Press, 1963.

Dank, B., 'Why homosexuals marry women', *Medical Aspects of Human Sexuality*, 1972 (August), 15-23.

Dannecker, M. and Reiche, R., *Der Gewöhnliche Homosexuelle: Eine Soziologische Untersuchung uber Mannliche Homosexuelle in der Bundesrepublik*, Frankfurt am Main: S. Fischer Verlag, 1974.

Davison, G. C., 'Homosexuality: the ethical challenge', *Journal of Consulting and Clinical Psychology*, 1976, *44*, 157-62.

Davison, G. C., 'Politics, ethics and therapy for homosexuality', *American Behavioral Psychologist*, 1982, *25*, 423-34.

Dean, R. B. and Richardson, H., 'Analysis of MMPI profiles of forty college-educated overt male homosexuals', *Journal of Consulting Psychology*, 1964, *28*, 483-6.

Denholtz, M. S., 'Extension of covert procedures in the treatment of male homosexuals', *Journal of Behavior Therapy and Experimental Psychiatry*, 1973, *4*, 305.

Dickey, B. A., 'Attitudes towards sex roles and feelings of adequacy in homosexual males', *Journal of Consulting Psychology*, 1961, *25*, 116-22.

Evans, R. B., 'Review of Weinberg, M. S. and Williams, C. J., 'Male homosexuals: their problems and adaptations', *Journal of Homosexuality*, 1974, *1*, 127-30.

Gagnon, J. H. and Simon, W., *Sexual Conduct: The Sources of Human Sexuality*, Chicago: Aldine, 1973.

Green, R., 'Sexual identity of 37 children raised by homosexual or transsexual parents', *American Journal of Psychiatry*, 1978, *135*, 692-7.

Hooker, E., 'The adjustment of the male overt homosexual', *Journal of Projective Techniques*, 1957, *21*, 18-31.

Hooker, E., 'An empirical study of some relations between sexual patterns and gender identity in male homosexuals', in Money, J. (ed), *Sex Research: New Developments*, New York: Holt, Rinehart & Winston, 1965.

Humphreys, R. A. L., *Tearoom Trade* London: Duckworth, 1970.

References

Imieliński, K., 'Homosexuality in males with particular reference to marriage', *Psychotherapy and Psychosomatics*, 1969, *17*, 126-32.

Kelman, H. C., 'Processes of opinion change', *Public Opinion Quarterly*, 1961, *25*, 57-8.

Kinsey, A. C., Pomeroy, W. B. and Martin, C. E., *Sexual Behaviour in the Human Male*, Philadelphia: W. B. Saunders, 1948.

Latham, J. D. and White, G. D., 'Coping with homosexual expression within heterosexual marriages: five case studies', *Journal of Sex and Marital Therapy*, 1978, *4*, 198-212.

Lautmann, R., 'The pink triangle: the persecution of homosexual males in concentration camps in Nazi Germany', *Journal of Homosexuality*, 1980-1, *6* (1 & 2), 141-60.

Lazarus, R. S., *Personality* (2nd ed.), Englewood Cliffs: Prentice-Hall, 1971.

MacDonald, A. P., 'Identification and measurement of multidimensional attitudes toward equality between the sexes', *Journal of Homosexuality*, 1974, *1*, 165-82.

MacDonald, A. P., 'Bisexuality: some comments on research and theory', *Journal of Homosexuality*, 1981, *6* (3), 21-35.

MacDonald, A. P. and Games, R. G., 'Some characteristics of those who hold positive and negative attitudes toward homosexuals', *Journal of Homosexuality*, 1974, *1*, 9-27.

McKenzie, N., *Women in Australia*, Melbourne: Cheshire, 1962.

McNeill, J. J., *The Church and the Homosexual*, London: Darton, Longman & Todd, 1977.

Marshall, W. L., 'The modification of sexual fantasies: a combined treatment approach to the reduction of deviant sexual behaviour', *Behaviour Research and Therapy*, 1973, *11*, 557-64.

Masters, W. H. and Johnson, V. E., *Homosexuality in Perspective*, Boston: Little, Brown, 1979.

Miller, B., 'Adult sexual resocialisation: adjustments toward a stigmatised identity', *Alternative Lifestyles*, 1978, *1*, 207-34.

Miller, B., 'Unpromised paternity: lifestyles of gay fathers', in Levine, M. (ed), *Gay Men: The Sociology of Male Homosexuality*, New York: Harper & Row, 1979a.

Miller, B., 'Gay fathers and their children', *Family Co-ordinator*, 1979b, *28*, 544-52.

Neill, J. R., Marshall, J. R. and Yale, C. E., 'Marital changes after intestinal bypass surgery', *Journal of the American Medical*

Association, 1978, *240*, 447-50.

Noordhoff, J. E. (ed), *Sex in Nederland*, Utrecht: Prisma-boek, 1970.

Rehm, L. P. and Rozensky, R. H., 'Multiple behaviour therapy techniques with a homosexual client: a case study', *Journal of Behaviour Therapy and Experimental Psychiatry*, 1974, *5*, 53-7.

Richardson, D. and Hart, J., 'Married and isolated homosexuals', in Hart, J. and Richardson, D., *The Theory and Practice of Homosexuality*, London: Routledge & Kegan Paul, 1981.

Ross, H. L., 'Modes of adjustment of married homosexuals', *Social Problems*, 1971, *18*, 385-93.

Ross, H. L., 'Odd couples: homosexuals in heterosexual marriages', *Sexual Behaviour*, 1972, *2* (7), 42-9.

Ross, M. W., 'Relationships between sex role and sex orientation in homosexual men', *New Zealand Psychologist*, 1975, *4* (1), 25-9.

Ross, M. W., 'Paradigm lost or paradigm regained? Behaviour therapy and homosexuality', *New Zealand Psychologist*, 1977, *6* (1), 42-51.

Ross, M. W., 'The relationship of perceived societal hostility, conformity and psychological adjustment in homosexual men', *Journal of Homosexuality*, 1978, *4*, 157-68.

Ross, M. W., 'Heterosexual marriage of homosexual males: some associated factors', *Journal of Sex and Marital Therapy*, 1979, *5*, 142-51.

Ross, M. W., 'Bisexuality: fact or fallacy?', *British Journal of Sexual Medicine*, 1979, *6* (45), 49-50.

Ross, M. W., 'Retrospective distortion in homosexual research', *Archives of Sexual Behaviour*, 1980, *9*, 523-31.

Ross, M. W., 'Societal influences on gender role in homosexuals: a cross-cultural comparison', *Journal of Sex Research*, 1983a, *19* (1), in press.

Ross, M. W., 'Societal reaction, adjustment and homosexuality measurement in two societies', *Journal of Sex Research*, 1983b, *19*, in press.

Ross, M. W., Rogers, L. J. and McCulloch, H., 'Stigma, sex and society: a new look at gender differentiation and sexual variation', *Journal of Homosexuality*, 1978, *3*, 315-30.

Ross, M. W. and Talikka, A., 'Finland and homosexuality', *Psychiatric News*, 1978, *13* (14), 2 & 10.

Ross, M. W. and Talikka, A., 'Homosexual labelling and cultural control', *Psychiatric Opinion*, 1979, *16* (10), 31-3.

Rotter, J. B., 'Generalised expectancies for internal versus external control of reinforcement', *Psychological Monographs*, 1966, *80* (1), whole no. 609.

Russell, A. and Winkler, R., 'Evaluation of assertive training and homosexual guidance service groups designed to improve homosexual functioning', *Journal of Consulting and Clinical Psychology*, 1977, *45*, 1-13.

Saghir, M. T. and Robins, E., *Male and Female Homosexuality: A Comprehensive Investigation*, Baltimore: Williams & Wilkins, 1973.

Serber, M. and Keith, C. G., 'The Atascadero Project: model of a sexual retaining program for incarcerated homosexual pedophiles', *Journal of Homosexuality*, 1974, *1*, 87-97.

Sherif, M.,'A study of some social factors in perception', *Archives of Psychology*, 1935, *187*.

Shively, M. and DeCecco, J. P., 'Components of sexual identity', *Journal of Homosexuality*, 1977, *3*, 41-8.

Silverstein, C. and White, E., *The Joy of Gay Sex: An Intimate Guide for Gay Men to the Pleasures of a Gay Lifestyle*, New York: Crown, 1977.

Simon, W. and Gagnon, J. H., 'Homosexuality: the formulation of a sociological perspective', *Journal of Health and Social Behaviour*, 1967, *8*, 179-85.

Stern, M. and Stern, A., *Sex in the Soviet Union*, London: W. H. Allen, 1981.

Townes, B. D., Ferguson, W. D. and Gillam, S., 'Differences in psychological sex, adjustment, and familial influences among homosexual and nonhomosexual populations', *Journal of Homosexuality*, 1976, *1*, 261-72.

Wafelbakker, F., 'Marriages of homosexuals', *British Journal of Sexual Medicine*, 1975, *2* (4), 18-21.

Weinberg, M. S., 'The male homosexual: Age related variations in social and psychological characteristics', *Social Problems*, 1970, *17*, 527-37.

Weinberg, M. S. and Williams, C. J., *Male Homosexuals: Their Problems and Adaptations*, New York: Oxford, 1974.

Wilson, G. D. (ed), *The Psychology of Conservatism*, London: Academic Press, 1973.

Wolfenden, J. (Chairman), *Report of the Committee on Homosexual Offences and Prostitution*, London: HMSO, 1957.

Index

Index